Letters from the Mayflower
Dorothy May Bradford

Written by E.W. Robertson

in honor of the 400th anniversary of
the *Mayflower* voyage

*To Bill,
Enjoy the story!
Libby Robertson
2020*

E.W. Robertson
Letters from the *Mayflower*: Dorothy May Bradford
Copyright © 2020, E.W. Robertson

Cover and book design
R.L. Robertson

Cover painting: William Formby Halsall (1841-1919)
The Mayflower on Her Arrival in Plymouth Harbor, circa 1882.
Oil on canvas.

Printed in the United States of America

ISBN 978-1-7923-4112-0

Published by the author
libbyrobertson331@gmail.com

To my sisters

Acknowledgements

Letters from the Mayflower was written in recognition of the upcoming 400th anniversary of the amazing *Mayflower* journey. An enormous debt of gratitude is owed to the men, women, and children who made the epic journey. They gave their lives. They gave their all. They did it for their children. They did it to prepare a way for all those who might follow. They did it in trust and full obedience to bring the gospel of Jesus Christ to foreign shores.

I am grateful for the inheritance of faith that the passengers and their families have passed down through the generations. I admire those who dedicate their lives to studying the genealogies and historical records of this significant and unique event in our history.

Many thanks to my husband, children, friends, and family who encouraged me in this creative endeavor.

Special thanks to the team at Eschler Editing for insights in developing the story.

Last of all, but most of all, I thank Jesus who makes himself known. He guided and directed this creative journey.

Author's Note

He that hath an ear, let him hear what the Spirit saith unto the churches;
To him that overcometh will I give to eat of the tree of life, which is in the midst
of the paradise of God.
— Revelation 2:7

God leads in mysterious ways.

Our typical Thanksgiving family meal includes turkey and mashed potatoes, green beans and corn, dressing and noodles—all of the traditional holiday favorites plus an occasional new recipe or two. There's always too much food for one family to consume in one sitting. We gather—parents, grandparents, siblings, nieces, nephews, aunts, uncles, stepchildren, their children, sometimes guests, as many as can fit around the table—for an amazing feast of lively conversation and fabulous foods.

At a recent Thanksgiving celebration, in between the passing of rolls and butter and the salt and pepper, my brother-in-law started telling us about a fascinating book he was reading called *Mayflower: A Story of Courage, Community, and War*. It was a timely conversational item, and we listened intently as he described the dangers and extreme circumstances the Pilgrims faced in journeying to and establishing their colony.

It made me keenly aware of the debt of gratitude owed to those families for their establishment of Christianity and the Christian faith in America, for what they went through, and for their courage, faith, and determination. I needed to be thankful for their perseverance and travail. Much like missionaries of my day, they intended to advance the Christian faith and were willing to follow wherever God led—first fleeing England to the safety of Holland, then leaving everything and everyone they knew in Holland to start a new life in an uncivilized, unpopulated, completely unknown land. Their unique obedience brought the gospel to the shores of Cape Cod, and then their trust, their belief, and the power of Almighty God kept that faith alive as it passed down through the generations and eventually found its way to me.

I was intrigued to learn more about these Pilgrims, their risks, their courage, their obedience, their story. I borrowed my brother-in-law's book, and my first read was eye-opening. I knew the fundamentals: the Pilgrims sailed on the *Mayflower* in 1620 in pursuit of religious freedom; they wrote the Mayflower Compact; they landed at Plymouth Rock; they made friends with the Indians, who helped them celebrate the first Thanksgiving. But I knew nothing about them as individuals. I had grown up knowing *of* them but had no understanding of the depth of their faith or the struggles they encountered while traveling to America.

I became fascinated with these 102 passengers—men, women, and young children—who put their lives on the line to follow a dream. I was stunned that my initial research uncovered little about the actual journey and even less material about the *Mayflower* women. Did all the kudos belong to the men? Didn't the women play a vital role in enduring the hardships of the voyage, in establishing the community that gave shape to our great country, in developing relationships with the natives? Were these women (three of whom were pregnant at the time) only spectators to history in the making? These women were deeply grounded in their love and trust of the Lord, faithful to him in the midst of extreme and horrific conditions. To give life to their view, their strength, their courage, and their joy became a goal of mine in the telling of this story.

Through my readings of the incredible conviction of these passengers, I was truly captivated by Dorothy May Bradford. She emerged as an adventurous, bright, capable woman with an energetic, pioneer spirit who was focused on God's promises. I see her as an unsung hero, a bold young woman, strong in mind, strong in spirit, strong in character. While Dorothy no doubt had personal challenges, I believe she kept personal enemies, like discouragement and fear, in check. Armed with all the characteristics of biblical goodness and insight, Dorothy is an inspiring example of courage in the face of dramatic circumstances. I see her as a fearless believer, always hopeful, and as an amazingly positive woman of perseverance and faith.

Letters from the Mayflower is inspired by historical events, facts and actual persons, but it is a work of fiction. While some of the events that Dorothy writes of actually occurred, the letters themselves, and all content in the letters, are a creation of my imagination, based on my research, and written from Dorothy's perspective.

— E.W. Robertson

Meet the Passengers

*That in blessing I will bless thee, and in multiplying I will multiply thy seed
as the stars of the heaven, and as the sand which is upon the sea shore; and thy
seed shall possess the gate of his enemies;*
*And in thy seed shall all the nations of the earth be blessed; because thou
has obeyed my voice.*
— Genesis 22:17–18

There are limited firsthand accounts of *Mayflower's* voyage, but snippets
of history provide the remarkable story. In addition to the twenty-six members
of the ship's crew, the ship carried 102 passengers: fifty-one men, twenty-
one boys, twenty women, and ten girls, in addition to two dogs and a handful
of domestic farm animals. These passengers included entire families, single
parents, children, orphans, servants, a self-taught physician, a preacher, a soldier, a troublemaker, a cooper, a weaver, a tailor, a shoemaker, a negotiator,
three pregnant women, and one man who had been to America before.

More than half of the passengers were from Pastor John Robinson's Pu-
ritan congregation in Leiden, Holland. They held strong beliefs and sought
religious freedom. Other families, from the mainland of England, had little
or no religious sentiments. Not one had experience in building a community
from scratch, yet all passengers hoped to eventually own land and provide a
fresh start for their families in the New World.

Passengers from Pastor Robinson's congregation were part of a move-
ment that had roots dating back to the sixteenth and seventeenth centuries,
when the Church of Rome was transformed into a state Church of England.
These Puritans believed that many of the church's imposed practices had no
actual biblical foundation. Striving to stay true to the Bible as their guide to
daily life, they separated from the national church in the early 1600s. For this
they faced persecution, and by 1607 many had abandoned their homeland,
seeking refuge across the English Channel in Holland, where they could worship as they pleased.[1]

This was a good solution for many years. Yet some, in particular Pastor
Robinson's congregation, believed even the haven they found in Holland was
not enough. His close-knit congregation grew increasingly restless, alarmed by
the worldliness around them and pressures to conform to the Dutch ways of
life. Their calling was to America, a New World, where they could start fresh
in a community all their own and follow religious practices as they saw fit.

Pastor Robinson's congregation would not be intimidated by the horror stories of the struggling Jamestown colony.[2] Instead they sought God's direction, and by June 1619, congregation leaders had taken steps to finalize negotiations with the Virginia Company, an enterprise working to establish settlements along the coast of America. These church leaders secured a patent that gave the group the right to form a colony in America within five to seven years. The congregation planned to capitalize on the rich resources of America; they would fish the shores and trade in furs until such a time when they could apply for an additional patent to claim the land as their own.

By spring of 1620 nearly a third of the congregation members were prepared and anxious to depart. Others would follow soon after. In order to reach America before winter, they hastily completed the final steps: purchasing a small boat to be used for fishing and exploring, purchasing a seaworthy vessel (the *Speedwell*), hiring a shipmaster (Master Reynolds), and organizing their departure from the nearby port of Delfshaven. They would sail to England; meet up with the Londoners (families joining from the mainland of England) and their ship, the *Mayflower*; then travel together to the claim of land at the mouth of the Hudson River. And so our story begins on the riverbanks of Delfshaven . . .

List of Characters

John Alden, a member of the *Mayflower's* crew, served as her cooper. He later decided to remain at Plymouth Colony with the other passengers.

Mary Norris Allerton was entering the third trimester of a pregnancy at the time of this journey. She traveled with her husband **Isaac Allerton** and their three children: **Bartholomew, Remember,** and **Mary.** Isaac was a prominent member of Pastor Robinson's congregation and became involved in the business decisions and dealings with the Virginia Company. Isaac's sister, Sarah Allerton, stayed behind in Leiden with her two young daughters, Mary and Sarah, but her husband, **Degory Priest,** traveled on the *Mayflower.*

Eleanor and **John Billington** came on the *Mayflower* with their two sons **John** and **Francis.**

Dorothy May Bradford was the daughter of Henry and Katherine May. In 1613 she married **William Bradford,** a leading member of Pastor Robinson's congregation. William was born in England, became an orphan by the age of seven, and was raised by his grandfather and then his uncle. He became associated with Pastor Robinson's congregation at an early age and followed them from England to Holland in 1607. Dorothy and William settled, along with the rest of the congregation, in the community of Leiden. Their son John was born in 1617. Little John did not make the trip with his parents on the *Mayflower* but stayed behind; he would be sent for later once the colony was established. Little John likely lived in Holland with Dorothy's family, which at the time consisted of her mother and her sister Jaqueline (apparently her father died around 1617). In 2017 it was discovered that Dorothy was the niece of passenger William White, half-brother to Dorothy's father Henry.[3] Dorothy's fictional letters are written to her sister Jaqueline.

Mary Brewster traveled with her husband **William Brewster**, preacher and ruling elder of the congregation, and their two sons **Love** and **Wrestling**. To make a living in Leiden, William Brewster taught English to students at the university. He also partnered with Thomas Brewer and Edward Winslow to run a printing press that published religious books and pamphlets that spoke out against the English government. The Brewsters left three of their older children behind: Jonathan, Patience, and Fear. The older children planned to come to America with the rest of the congregation.

Peter Browne traveled as an apprentice to the Mullins family.

Katherine White Carver was a prominent woman in the Leiden congregation. She was sister to Bridget Robinson, wife of the congregation's pastor. Katherine's husband **John Carver** was a church deacon and one of the chief negotiators for the congregation as they secured a patent for land with the Virginia Company. He was in charge of purchasing supplies for the voyage. He was chosen as the first governor of the Plymouth Colony once the ship arrived in America.

Mrs. (first name unknown) and **James Chilton** of Leiden traveled with their youngest daughter **Mary**. James is known as the oldest *Mayflower* passenger. Mary was 13 years old and is known as the first female to step ashore at Plymouth.

Robert Coppin assisted Master Jones in sailing the *Mayflower*.

Richard Clarke was a *Mayflower* passenger.

John Crackstone of Leiden and his young son **John** were *Mayflower* passengers.

Robert Cushman was a key businessman who returned to Leiden after the *Speedwell* was abandoned.

Sarah and **Francis Eaton** of Leiden traveled with their one-year-old son **Samuel**.

Dr. Samuel Fuller, a self-taught physician, was a longtime member and deacon of the congregation. He left his wife, Bridget, and his one-year-old daughter behind in Leiden and brought a young servant with him named **William Butten**. Dr. Fuller's brother **Edward** was also from Leiden and traveled with his **wife** (first name unknown) and young son **Samuel**.

John Goodman was a member of the Leiden congregation and traveled with two dogs, an English Spaniel and a female mastiff.

John Hooke of Norwich, England, came on the *Mayflower* as servant to the Allertons.

Elizabeth Fisher Hopkins gave birth to baby **Oceanus** during the journey. Her husband **Stephen Hopkins** was the only passenger who had been to America before. They traveled with their three other children: **Constance**, **Giles** and **Damaris**.

John Howland of Fenstanton, England, came on the *Mayflower* as servant to the Carvers.

Master Christopher Jones was the shipmaster of the *Mayflower*.

Edward Leister was a servant traveling with the Hopkins family.

Mary Prower Martin traveled with her son **Solomon Prower** and her husband **Christopher Martin** who assisted with purchasing supplies for the journey, then served as governor of the *Speedwell*.

Desire Minter was a young girl who traveled as a servant to the Carvers. She was the daughter of William and Sarah Willet Minter. Sarah was midwife for the Leiden church.

The More Children: The children's nonbiological father, Samuel More, was wed to their mother, Katherine, in 1610. After their fourth child was born, Samuel proclaimed openly that none of the four children were his. He accused Katherine of an affair and sought separation, and she lost custody of the children. He revoked the children's inheritance and arranged to have them shipped to Virginia. The children were taken to London and handed over to Robert Cushman and Thomas Weston until such a time when they could be placed on the *Mayflower*. **Ellen**, age eight, became an indentured servant to the Winslows. **Jasper**, age seven, became an indentured servant to the Carvers. **Richard**, age six, and **Mary**, age four, became indentured servants to the Brewsters.

Alice and **William Mullins** of Dorking, England, traveled with their children **Priscilla** and **Joseph** and left behind their two oldest children, Sarah and William.

Master Reynolds was the shipmaster of the *Speedwell*.

Alice and **John Rigsdale** were among the oldest *Mayflower* passengers.

Rose Standish traveled with her husband, **Myles Standish**, an English soldier.

Elias Story was a servant traveling with Edward Winslow.

John Robinson was pastor of the Separatist congregation. He and his wife Bridget stayed behind in Leiden with the majority of the church's congregation.

Thomas Rogers was a member of the Leiden church congregation and traveled with his oldest son **Joseph**. He left his wife, Alice, and three children, John, Elizabeth and Margaret, behind in Leiden.

Edward Thompson was a servant traveling with William White.

Agnes Cooper Tilley traveled with her husband **Edward Tilley**, her nephew **Henry Samson** (son of Agnes's sister Martha), and her niece **Humility Cooper** (daughter of Agnes's brother Robert). They were joined by Edward's brother **John Tilley**, his wife **Joan Hurst Tilley**, and their daughter **Elizabeth**.

Jane (history records her first name as unknown, but possibly Jane) and **Thomas Tinker** were passengers along with their **son** (first name also unknown).

John Turner was a member of the Leiden church congregation. He traveled with his **two sons**.

Thomas Weston was a merchant who organized financial backing for the colonists.

Susanna Jackson White gave birth to baby boy **Peregrine** while the *Mayflower* was anchored in Cape Cod Bay. She traveled with her husband **William White** and five-year-old son **Resolved**.

Elizabeth Barker Winslow traveled with her husband **Edward Winslow**, who moved from England to Leiden around 1617 to join Pastor Robinson's congregation. Edward was a leading member of the congregation and helped William Brewster with his underground printing.

The Mayflower at Sea

Saturday, July 22, 1620

Jesus saith unto him, I am the way, the truth, and the life: no man cometh unto the Father, but by me.
— John 14:6

My dear sister Jaqueline,

So many tears shed today as we set sail from Delfshaven. We've been preparing for this day for weeks now, so you'd think we'd have been better rehearsed at goodbyes, but leaving all of you behind is much more difficult than I ever imagined.

William and I stayed on the ship's deck for a long time, watching and waving until you disappeared from our sight. Then, when we could no longer see land, I tried to lock an image of each of you in my mind for as long as possible. You are all so precious to us.

Thank you for your help in trying to make light of our departure, for little John's sake. His waving and jumping up and down brings a smile to me now. He seemed so pleased to see us in the big boat. He does love boats. I hope you will continue reading to him of boats and faraway places. We've spared him no detail of our journey to America: the boat, the wild lands, the new home we will build. His adventuresome smile seemed especially bright this morning. But all I can think of now are his sweet blond curls, which I love to wrap in my fingers.

If the day has been typical, he is hatching from an afternoon nap. I love how his first stretch and yawn are with both eyes closed. After a bit he will stretch again with one eye open as if to make note of anything he might have missed while sleeping. Then, when he catches me looking, that smile fills the room. Hug him tightly for both William and me.

I imagine by now you have shared the first of the "surprise" packages we left behind for him. The one you were to give him at noon today is by far his favorite snack—we made the strawberry filling together a couple days ago, and he kept asking what we were going to use it for. Now he knows! Hope that brings a smile to his face. His bedtime gift is a tiny fabric ball that William made. It's small enough to hold while he sleeps, and he can carry it in his pocket during the day if he wants.

No doubt you and Momma will spoil him rotten. But staying behind with you truly is the perfect place for him and a comfort for us. I am pleased also that many friends from Leiden are willing to give you a rest now and then. I'm not sure how that will be possible, but it is a lovely offer.

Momma looked so frail today. I could tell that she hasn't been sleeping well. Her eyes, red and puffy, took me by surprise, which was completely my fault. I should have been prepared to comfort her. In spite of our tears, I am thankful for her blessing and that we had our goodbyes on good terms. I know she is not happy about our leaving.

Does she sense, as I do, that I have picked up her cross of faith and made it my own? Does she understand that in making this journey, I am our family's representative, so in a sense I am making this journey for her? She may not be physically with me on this boat, but she is here in spirit, in an enormous way. It is only because of her example that I am even able to travel this far from home. She certainly knows the importance of this journey and settlement for continuing to grow the Kingdom.

I pray you are a comfort to her when she is burdened with worry and concern, as those mental enemies will most certainly come to discourage her. Remind her that I am not far in spirit and that it is with pride, as her daughter, that I have taken this step. I would not be here without the faith that she and Poppa both instilled within me, the courage to go where God leads, wherever that may be. I hope she is able to stay strong. I will cling to the hope that she, too, might be able to join us—I can't even imagine how wonderful if we could all be reunited in Virginia.

I am reminded of the story of Simon from Cyrene. There he was, heading into Jerusalem from the country. Soldiers picked him out of the crowd to carry that heavy cross. In the flurry of a moment, he had to walk away from his family. And he had no choice but to go. Did he have a wife and children who cried as he left? Did they quietly watch in horror, afraid because of the soldiers? I imagine he met up with his family later that day. Surely they followed him, but you know, it changed their plans for the day and changed their lives for eternity. You can imagine none of them were ever the same. Was that all somehow part of God's plan for their lives?

I very much feel that way. Although no one is demanding us to make this journey, it is clearly God's calling. So, we pick up and go and follow. But in our obedience to God there is a cost to other people, and that is where the anguish comes. I love my Lord, and my obedience to him is pure delight. True, this journey and leaving little John and all of you behind upsets the normal path a family takes. But if I disobey to prevent the suffering, I know we will all pay the cost. I can only trust that God knows best and pray his mighty hands will hold you safe until we are together again.

Still, it goes against every fiber of my mothering instinct to leave little John for this amount of time. I haven't been without him for more than a couple hours at a time since the day he was born. He has been a part of my daily routine, all day long, and now I have to figure out how to live without him for a time, have to learn to live without all of you for at least a season or two. I know it is best for him to gain strength and make the trip with you next year. I must keep remembering that. . .and keep focused on the fact that we are going ahead to prepare a place for him and for you.

It's just that sometimes those motherly instincts allow doubts to come flooding in—am I doing this for selfish reasons, to satisfy some deep, personal desire for wild adventure? Or am I following God's calling? Some have been critical and say I'm abandoning God's true purpose for my life, that my first calling was to motherhood before talk of America came up, and so caring for my boy should be my number one priority. And then I find that while following God's call is the only choice I really have, this calling to America comes at great expense to you, my family, and friends. What a burden I've placed on you, to care for a child in these times, to feed an extra family member when money is scarce, to pick up the extra responsibility of a young boy while you have your own life to attend to. I have to ask myself, "Would I have done the same for you?" I would hope so but am not completely confident with my answer.

In spite of my confidence in God's plan, I am anxious and even now am finding it hard to hold back tears. Leiden has been a haven for our church for almost seven years, so it was more difficult than expected to finally say goodbye. When we were welcomed nowhere else, we found shelter and friends there. And while we have good and godly reasons for leaving, it has proven to be a fine home for our families. Even though I've learned that to say goodbye for a time doesn't necessarily mean forever, it is hard to think about those I won't see for a long while.

I remember when we left Cambridgeshire many years ago.[4] I thought I would not see many family members ever again, but one by one, our uncles, aunts, cousins, friends, and families from childhood also found their way to Amsterdam, and we had many pleasant and sweet reunions. Then, when I married William and we moved to Leiden, I again thought I might never again see you and Momma, but it turned out with only a day's journey between us, we have had many numerous occasions of joyful family celebrations. If I've learned anything about following God's leading, it's that life is full of surprises. There might be some I said goodbye to today whom I will not see again. But some will no doubt surprise me one day and show up unexpected on my door. My hope and prayer is that you will be the first of them. It is all part of God's strange and amazing plan. This journey is the next step in God's leading for my life.

Can you tell already that this writing tablet will be my saving grace? I thank you now from the depths of my heart, for it was a very thoughtful gift. When I have free time I will write as much as I possibly can for you of the details of this journey. I want you to know it all. And may I remind you I am expecting the same from you—a full record of little John's growth and changes and any life moments that I will miss out on over the next several months. Then, when you join us next spring, we can compare notes and share all our thoughts from being apart.

I know you are leery of the written word; I can hear you now. "Anyone can write anything, so how do you know what to believe?" I also know that my heart has been touched, inspired by many a written word. In some cases, I owe much gratitude to those who have taken the time to write. So, I am encouraged here to do the same, to share honest thoughts, be them good or not so lovely. I see this as an opportunity to record God's hand at work as we journey to America.

Our home for the next month is as tiny a space as William and I have ever shared. We laugh now about our little group of homes in the Leiden alley. Our front room was simple and provided plenty of space for us to cook and eat and play; that huge open hearth was a cozy spot to read to little John before bedtime. There are things I will miss about that house: the low fieldstone wall on the side yard, weathered and leisurely draped beside the walkway to hide those prickly shrubs; our garden, which will no doubt soon be overflowing with the fullness of summer—orange carrots, red turnips, sweet potatoes, and barley; the small white fenced section by the front door where we could sit and wave to folks walking by. I have vivid pictures of that house in my mind. To think we considered it small in comparison to other homes nearby. It served us well for seven years, but I'm telling you true, Jaqueline, that I have never known "small" as what we have in these current quarters. There was little privacy in the alley, but there is absolutely no privacy here. Praise God it is only temporary. I will keep telling myself that. I am not complaining, mind you, but wanting to portray a full picture for you of our experience here.

We are all crammed into what they call the gun deck, or between deck.

Our barrels and crates, chests and tools, and spare equipment and supplies are all in storage in the cargo hold below, and the work area on the main deck is mostly reserved for the ship's crew, so the passengers will hole up in the "between" for the length of our journey. It is literally overflowing with people and possessions: chests of clothing, small barrels of food, chairs, pillows, bedding, rugs, chamber pots, and firearms. It is worthy to note what our friends chose to bring with them. Some have a priority of shoes, scarves, hats, cooking supplies, linens. Every family seems to have a different focus. Mary Brewster brought her William's favorite chair and bench. John Goodman, one of our younger congregation members, brought his faithful English spaniel. It is easy to see that William and I treasure the power of the written word; our priority is books. We chose to safely tuck books into the sides of our storage trunks and carefully placed books into every nook and cranny, every crack and crevice of our family crate. Recipe books. Poetry books. Books by Shakespeare, John Donne, Martin Luther, John Calvin. And every book written by Pastor Robinson. I have one Bible in my bunk and one Bible—the one from Momma and Poppa—is in our storage crate below. I also have the book of hours, which I will read each day for encouragement.[5]

William and I have bunks, one above the other. The bunk is long enough for me to stretch my legs, but William's feet dangle over the edge. Momma's handmade quilted pillows add a cheerful splash of color to our otherwise dark and dreary bunks. And even though there is not an inch to spare, I of course found a spot for my box of treasures. It is my only connection now to you and little John. His darling sketch of the horse and chickens. His crumpled note with a red heart and his attempt at spelling "I love you." The flat, smooth stone from our last day at the river. A couple of coins from Poppa. A hankie from Grandmother. The tiny collection of rocks from Grandfather. Your sweet note of "goodbye for a time."

Thankfully, we are bunked next to Mary Brewster. She is anxious for her William to join us. We have had little word from him in over a year as he has been in London hiding from the authorities. She is hoping *and* expecting, based on what the church leaders have whispered in confidence, that he will join us at our first port in England. Mary has had her hands full these last few weeks, getting preparations readied for her and the two youngest boys. Their three older children—Jonathan, Patience, and Fear—were a help, but they made a choice to stay in Leiden with the rest of the congregation and thought it best to join our group next year. Mary is only hoping that her William will not be too upset by this arrangement.[6]

The Winslows are across from us. I imagine these accommodations leave much to be desired for them because they had one of the roomier homes in the alley. Edward Winslow is putting on his best sense of humor, though, and Elizabeth is delightful, so we've had much to speak about as we've settled into our spaces. They share their bunk area with two servants, so there is little room for that group.

I will write more but am needed to help with serving the meal.

All my love to you, dear sister, and to God be the glory!

Sunday, July 23

The Spirit of the Lord is upon me, because he hath anointed me to preach the gospel to the poor; he hath sent me to heal the brokenhearted, to preach deliverance to the captives, and recovering of sight to the blind, to set at liberty them that are bruised,
— Luke 4:18

My dear Jaqueline,

William and I stayed up late into the night talking, and I barely slept a wink; I could not stop thinking about our departure. The outpouring of neighbors, family, friends, and strangers that came to bid us farewell was astounding. Don't you agree? It seemed the entire town came to say goodbye. Even strangers we don't know lined the shore to wish us well. Do you think they were fascinated by our pursuit of religious freedom or perhaps our sense of adventure? Some, I am sure, think we're half-crazy. Did you see all those who followed us in their own boats to the mouth of the Channel, waving and singing and wishing us well? What a spectacle.

William was so touched by Pastor Robinson's goodbye speech on the deck. Were you able to hear that from where you stood? I can tell you his solemn words and prayer were a gift from God. As he read words from Ezra and fully commended our group into the Lord's hand, all sense of fear or doubt, all questions of how we will survive the journey or how we will establish the community, were completely washed away and replaced with the fullness of God's peace. What better gift?

Convinced we are that this *is* God's perfect plan and his perfect timing. Confident we are in his ability and power to see us safely to America's shores. I am sure there will be days ahead with doubts and questions, but I will always have that moment to go back to in my mind. That commendation was a defining moment. It brought a full sense of knowing that God's will is being done and that I am taking my proper place in his exciting purpose. It brings a sense of wonder to know that the Ruler of All was near and listening to the concerns of our tiny group. We are confident that God will graciously meet our needs as we carry this burden to establish a community of free worship. He has been building this passion within us for years, and to finally be on our way is beyond words.

The other thing that kept me awake last night is the still-troubling news of Pastor Robinson and Bridget choosing to stay behind. It simply does not make sense to me. William says I shouldn't let it bother me, so I am trying to trust their decision. But for me it raises doubts. It leads me to question whether or not we all should have waited until next spring. I don't like the idea of being separated from them. I suppose that Pastor Robinson will be an encouragement to the rest of the congregation during his extra time in Leiden. Perhaps he will convince even more to make this journey in the spring.

However, in a strange way it seems their decision to stay in Leiden for a while longer was a confirmation of our own decision to go. We are relieved to know that little John will have extra time to grow strong and healthy for the overseas journey and that you and our friends in Leiden will keep him busy all winter, focused on reading and studying God's Word. If anything, he will be spoiled rotten, living with you and Momma. We know you will keep him deeply rooted in family during this growing year.

Because we are in the calm waters of the Channel, Master Reynolds graciously allowed us space on deck for morning worship. You'll have to use your imagination to picture it. The upper deck, typically ruled by rough-edged sailors handling ropes and sails and knots, was completely quiet as Dr. Fuller read aloud the Word of our Lord. Although a founder of our congregation, Dr. Fuller lacks the experience of Elder Brewster and the education of Pastor Robinson, but since we are without both of them, the men requested Dr. Fuller lead today's service. He found a spot on the tallest step of the half deck; our group gathered below him on the platform between the half deck and the cook's room. What a sight.

We were singing, offering prayers and praise to God, and worshipping as we wanted, as free as the seagulls flying over us. No one came chasing after us. No one came pounding on the door. None of us had to hide or be fearful of imprisonment. This is why we came, Jaqueline. My heart was full of excitement.

Dr. Fuller's message was so appropriate—Hebrews 11:1. "Now faith is the substance of things hoped for, the evidence of things not seen." Don't you love that passage? Our faith is not in our ability to make this trip across the ocean. Our faith is in God and his power to carry us across this ocean, to carry out this plan for his Kingdom. I know that God has been faithful so many countless times in the past. He will provide us safe journey. He is the object of our faith and is ever so strong. He is able to do the impossible and sees infinitely more than we can ever imagine for this journey. Because of him, we are bound to see unimaginable glory.

Without any hymnals or instruments, it was a completely different experience of worship. The King's hymn took on new meaning for us; our voices lifted high and loud into the wind.

O Lord, the Maker of all things,
We pray thee now in this evening
Us to defend through thy mercy,
From all deceit of our enemy.
Let neither us deluded be,
Good Lord, with dream or phantasy,
Our heart waking in thee thou keep,
That we in sin fall not on sleep.
O Father, through thy blessed Son,
Grant us this our petition;
To whom with the Holy Ghost always
In heaven and earth be laud and praise.[7]

Won't Elder Brewster be excited? To experience this newfound freedom in worship will make every hardship he has faced seem trivial. And while there is no real way to know where all of this will lead, it is clear we can trust the God who oversees the course of the stars, the moon, the sun, and the planets. He is the one who has provided this freedom. He is the one who provides our food and friendships. He will oversee this adventure and bring these things to pass. This is what we hope for, and we are convinced of it.

After worship, we noticed the Channel was busy, so William and I found an out-of-the-way spot and stayed on deck. It is one thing to stay below at night when all is dark and quiet but quite another to stay below during the day when you know there is fresh air to breathe and blue skies to be seen from horizon to horizon. Some of the women prefer to stay below with their children, which would make sense. If little John were here with me, I'd likely spend most of my time below with the women and children, so I am thankful for the opportunity to experience the upper deck during our journey.

One look at this clear, blue sky and you would think it's a typical summer day. It's warm and sunny. It's July. Everything about it seems leisurely. But William reminded me we don't really have the luxury of calling any day typical anymore. At least not for a few months. Every day will bring something new and will not fall into any category labeled as typical. We must set aside all normal routines for a time, but we had to take a few moments to enjoy the clear blue sky.

A gentle summer breeze blew across the deck. Wispy white clouds splattered across the mile-high backdrop of blue. At one point the clouds perfectly aligned, multiple rows of white lines, perfectly matched in length, like discarded bones of a fish on a beach. Many clouds had no recognizable pattern or shape, floating fluffy formations that shifted and morphed in a lazy sea of blue. A bright, sunny, cheery day. Worthy of noting here for you.

William and I were fascinated by all the boats. Fishing boats, passenger boats, cargo boats—a sea of riggings and ropes, of flags and sails, of comings and goings. It was impossible to track who was going where and why.

The upper deck is no place for children running around. There are ropes and riggings, and only a skilled crewman would know which one is connected to what. These seamen seem experienced and steady and all business. Some work up on a higher deck, some work on the main deck with canvas and ropes and cargo, some run back and forth from one section to the other, some stand in place and yell orders. . . but I'm not sure exactly whom the orders are for. It's a bit chaotic, but they must love what they do.

Master Reynolds appears to be skilled, quite likable, and organized. His crew jumps at his orders, responding quickly to his good-natured commands. William says that some shipmasters can be stern, so I'm pleased that we will be two months with a jolly one. Plus, William says the entire crew has agreed to stay with us for the first year in America to lend an extra hand with getting us settled.

We are making good timing and are on schedule to meet our sister ship, the *Mayflower*. Those passengers are boarding in London, and we will rendezvous in Southampton. There continues to be a bit of concern about adding a group of strangers to not just our travels but our community as well. Some of them have strong ties to our group, but others are completely unknown. Can they be trusted? Before we left, Pastor Robinson pleaded with us to do everything we could to avoid conflict with the new group. He urged us not to judge or condemn any outside our main group. Oh, how I pray they are those of good influence and that God will grant us the open minds and kind hearts we will need.

I find it so interesting that God's not sending us to the New World with just our close-knit group. William and I had a long discussion about that last night. He is so wise and always helps me see things from a bigger perspective. He believes that God has good reason for us to be joined by this group of outsiders. He trusts it is part of God's mysterious plan.

I also find it interesting that we will not just be thrown into the community to start working together but will be a month or so at sea, side by side, which

is more than enough time to get to know each another, to learn of our similarities and our differences. If they are making the same sacrifices we are, leaving
family and friends for a new land, then we already have those similarities. I can
see that it will be helpful to have extra workers for settling our community in
the wilds. I'm praying they will be of good stock and sturdy hand.

But I wonder their reasons for leaving. Are they fleeing bad family situations? Are they like us and looking for a place to worship freely? Time will
tell, but I pray it will be a blessing for both our groups.

Please remind little John how much we love him. Please remind him of
the importance of what we've set out to do. I pray that God will keep his little
mind safe from doubts. I pray that he will never forget all we've told him, or,
God forbid, who we are. I pray it won't take you too long to settle into new
routines.

I'm hoping to sleep better tonight.

Monday, July 24

But as it is written, Eye hath not seen, nor ear heard, neither have entered into the heart of man, the things which God hath prepared for them that love him.
— 1 Corinthians 2:9

Sweetest sister,

This is just the beginning of the amazing sights we will see. Oh, how I wish you were here to share the view. It is a crystal-clear morning, and I have a perfect view to the south of the coastline of France. Rugged cliffs and sand dunes slope down to a gray and rocky beach. They are sprinkled with tufts of tall grass that are blown by the wind and appear to wave us on. What a proud countryside she is.

To the north is my first view of England since we moved to Holland almost ten years ago. The brilliant white Dover cliffs stretch for miles and miles, stunning and impressive; they are more spectacular than I imagined. Sheer cliffs of chalky white cascade down to the edge of the water, where they disappear beneath the waves. They boldly guard the Strait, keeping watch over the Channel and heralding the strength of England. In contrast to their stark white, streaks of black flint ripple throughout. Trees and shrubs dot the cliff-sides. We aren't close enough to make out the exact species, but I can see gulls and cliff birds making nests.

It seems somehow appropriate, God ordained if you may, to have this view of our homeland before we journey west. It provides us a time of reflection, a sense of closure of that chapter in our lives. However, I wasn't expecting to have mixed feelings. Even William says that many emotions are stirring for him. Although his departure from England was different from ours and it's been years since we left, we will likely always consider England our true home.[8] Even when we get settled in Virginia, I wonder when it will begin to feel like home. I'm not sure I'll ever be able to let go of the hold England has on my heart.

I have strong childhood memories full of colors and sights and smells, like red roses everywhere, even growing wild along the side of the road. Huge wide-open fields of green grass and hay bales. Sipping cream tea with you and Momma on the front steps. That's home to me.

At times I ache for our family members still there—their loyalty to the crown, their pride, their stubbornness, their inability to accept change. Now

I see England as a strange island, full of political struggles and civility, full of turmoil, full of growing hostility with other countries and growing immorality. Some say there is a sense that the world is literally falling apart. What does it all mean? Will God soon reach down and decide enough is enough and send the fire that we all know will come someday? Many are convinced that the end is near. I am still not so sure.

Sometimes I even wonder if God has positioned our group here to be the remnant that the apostle John speaks of in Revelation, the ones who will be left behind to carry God's Word if this broken world falls. I can tell you that in spite of the dangers of this journey, in spite of the dangers that lie ahead for us, I am so glad we have left. I know there are challenges ahead, but when Pastor Robinson used to read passages that described "wars and rumours of wars" (Matthew 24:6), they seemed all too real. Out here, away from it all, I'm not so sure it matters. The talk of Spain invading England and Holland, the rumors growing of wars that have already broken out—William is truly fearful of a coming war. When he mentions war, I hear myself saying, "I don't have time to think about what that might mean. Should I waste my time thinking of what might happen? It might never happen." If war breaks out and my time comes, then it's my time, and there's no reason to fret over these things. Even though the world around me may be falling apart, God has given me a peace within about all of that. He is my refuge. This journey is my refuge. Yes, we live in a broken world, but just think, if God opens a door for us in this New World, how wonderful it will be to worship as we want. I read God's Word and am filled with calmness.

It makes me realize that even I don't have a big enough dream to match God's dream for me. I don't have a clue where this is all leading. What I do know is that we are called to believe, called to go forth, called to be salt and light in the world. In order to follow him, I must let go and let God have control of every circumstance in my life. Like the wind that blows our ship through this English Channel, the wind of God's Holy Spirit leads me and guides me.

Wednesday, July 26

Then he answered and spake upon me, saying, This is the word of the Lord unto Zerubbabel, saying, Not by might, nor by power, but by my spirit, saith the Lord of hosts.
— Zechariah 4:6

Dear Jaqueline,

I must tell you that pulling into Southampton today and catching our first sight of the *Mayflower* was a magnificent treat. She is three times the size of the *Speedwell*, over one hundred feet in length. She has three large masts, six massive sails, a long beak bow, and miles and miles and miles of ropes and riggings. She seems extremely sturdy and will be quite an inspiration as the *Speedwell* follows her lead across the Atlantic. We are anchored next to her, and the ship's enormous size overwhelms me. She towers over us. I can only think of little John and his excitement of seeing this ship.

But the true highlight of the day was meeting up with Elder Brewster late this afternoon. Mary has been in tears ever since, but they are happy tears. Williams seems visibly relieved to finally have his friend and comrade with us again, and it is a great comfort to see that Elder Brewster doesn't seem to be affected at all by his year in hiding. He is full of tales. Day after day he played hide-and-seek with church officials, living the life of a fugitive on the run. God has truly been his hiding place and Elder Brewster will be safe from the authorities. His intelligence and warm heartedness are an encouragement to our entire group. It feels once again that we are united in our mission and all is well. A bit unexpectedly he brought four indentured servants on board—two will bunk with the Brewsters, one with the Winslows, and one with John and Katherine Carver.

The Carvers were a welcome sight indeed. They have been in Southampton since June, making final arrangements and purchasing supplies for our voyage. With no children of their own, they decided to bring six indentured servants. Can you imagine?

We were also pleased to see Captain Myles Standish among the *Mayflower* crowd. He is well acquainted with many in our congregation. He was originally an English soldier but served in Holland, where he became close friends with Pastor Robinson. He is slightly older than William but more stout in size than I remembered. In spite of that, William is thrilled we will now have a delegate to take charge of our colony's defenses, one who can organize our men into a battalion if that is needed and can lead our explorations as we seek a place to build.

Apparently, the men had considered Captain John Smith for this very position. He is well-known for his experiences in settling the Virginia colonies. That would have been a boon, but William said we didn't have the resources to pay for his services. Standish was more affordable and more amenable to our religious preferences, so we are in good position there. We are especially pleased he brought his wife, Rose. She is the kindest of persons and seems to have a humorous way about her. She seems a perfect match to be married to such an adventurer. Her experience and wisdom in journeys will be a comfort for all the women, I'm sure.

We haven't had a chance yet to meet any of the other *Mayflower* passengers. I waved at some of them as they stood on their upper deck. For some reason our Master Reynolds has requested all the women and children to stay on board, and he is not letting any of the *Mayflower* passengers on to visit. The men have been free to disembark and exchange stories, but the rest of us have had to stay where we are. It is unfair, but I'm trying to hold my tongue. Doesn't he realize we'll be healthier and happier if we get a chance for a short walk and some interaction? I think he's afraid we'll get lost. He's obviously not used to accommodating women on his boats. Not that he's offensive or belittling, but as I've learned earlier today, the women may be the least of his worries.

As it turns out, the *Speedwell* has been taking on water since the Holland departure. Master Reynolds and crew are now even claiming the ship may be unseaworthy. Winslow happened to hear of it quite by accident last night. He immediately came to see William about the issue, and they spoke quietly of it late into the evening. Not a peep has been shared with the other families. I only know of this because Elizabeth and I were knitting and overheard their whispers. William knows me well and mentioned it before we drifted off to sleep last night. He didn't share all the details, but I bless him for the insight; he has learned in our years together that it's sometimes good for me to have advance warning of concerns. It provides me time to adjust to news so I can sort through scary details privately before needing to show a face of strength and courage for others. William will share this news with Elder Brewster, and at some point, they will have to discuss it with the full group, but for now we are not to mention this until the time is right. They won't know the full extent of the trouble for a day or two, but it seems very serious. They are looking into needed repairs. At least we made it safely to Southampton. God will provide for all of our needs.

Thursday, July 27

Hear therefore, O Israel, and observe to do it; that it may be well with thee, and that ye may increase mightily, as the Lord God of thy fathers hath promised thee, in the land that floweth with milk and honey.
— Deuteronomy 6:3

Dear Jaqueline,

I had a dream about Poppa in my waking hours, and my mind has been flooded with thoughts and images of him all morning. I didn't actually see him in my dream—just his huge, strong hands marked with age spots, hands that completely enveloped mine. His wonderful smile and gentle voice always warmed my heart. There are times I miss him so much and wish we could have even one more conversation together.

Poppa was convinced God had a purpose and a plan for the English to settle the Virginia shores. I remember him saying that just like God had chosen Caleb and Joshua to settle in the land of Canaan, he would raise up those to go into the new country. And here I am, Jaqueline; it's as if long ago Poppa spoke this journey into reality.

It's funny and frightening at the same time, but I have a sense of adventure in my blood. It's like a calling to lean on God at his Word, even in my days of doubt, to take good courage, to not be afraid or terrified of anything I encounter. It's a desire to see new places and try new things. Sometimes it's almost dreadful to recognize it as it wells up inside me and can't be held down. I have seen God go before us many times. I have seen him prove his faithfulness, and now I am bound to go. God has his mighty hand at work here and will safely establish our colony in the new country. I am confident of it. I pray that same sense of adventure, of boldness, will stay healthy and strong in you and that you will join me soon. Oh, how I wish Poppa were here to witness this. Although somehow, from the dream I had of him this morning, I sense that he is right here with me after all.

Friday, July 28

But in every thing by prayer and supplication with thanksgiving let your requests be made known unto God.

And the peace of God, which passeth all understanding, shall keep your hearts and minds through Christ Jesus.

— Philippians 4:6–7

Dear Jaqueline,

We are only one week into this journey, and there is already much discontent on the ship. Men are arguing. Women and children are restless to get moving. There are costs of repair work for the *Speedwell*, and we have had to sell precious supplies to get the work done. Then we have Thomas Weston and Christopher Martin debating with Carver and Robert Cushman.[9] Weston can't control his tone in any discussions that I've overheard and calls Cushman a scoundrel. He says there is nothing ahead for us but mismanagement and violence. I do have a great deal of respect for Cushman, but he is a gloomy sort. He wants nothing to do with Weston and his plans. He has been so dedicated to the success of our journey. For over a year now he has worked tirelessly to secure our supplies and provisions. But perhaps it has been too much for him. He seems highly stressed, to the point of being unhealthy.

It's too much for me. I am refusing to join into their conversations and am using my letters to you as my means of escape. Ha! Do I feel guilty about that? Not in the least. If a few minutes out of my day spent writing keeps me sane while on this insane voyage, I think no one would keep me from it. I take a deep breath and find my peace—peace where there was chaos and disorder, calm where there was panic and pandemonium, something where there was nothing, strength where there was emptiness and anxiety.

Sunday, July 30

Finally, my brethren, be strong in the Lord, and in the power of his might.

Put on the whole armour of God, that ye may be able to stand against the wiles of the devil.

For we wrestle not against flesh and blood, but against principalities, against powers, against the rulers of the darkness of this world, against spiritual wickedness in high places.

Wherefore take unto you the whole armour of God, that ye may be able to withstand in the evil day, and having done all, to stand.

— Ephesians 6:10–13

Dear Jaqueline,

I'll start by saying that morning services on deck were refreshing, and the slight breeze from the west was as encouraging as Elder Brewster's message. He was in his full element, and we soaked up every word of inspiration. Oh, how good it is to have him among us again.

William and I are resting below, and we are in the thick of summer. It is hotter than hot. William doesn't mind the heat. He prefers it over a cold, winter day, but the heat of summer always puts me a bit on edge. Here we are, stuck in port, while the *Speedwell* is being retrimmed.

Of course, I expect frustrations throughout this journey so in my prayers I have claimed God's authority over every detail of our travels, but let me describe this current situation in more detail for you. Unpleasant, uncomfortable, wasteful, annoying—there are a few words for you. The air is stagnant, heavy with moisture. Many are complaining. The day seems long, and time is moving slower than slow. All I can look forward to today are evening services back up on deck. I wish again we had started our journey on schedule as planned— had we left in May we might already be in Virginia with building underway.

What is most frustrating to me is that every delay in departure means a delay in arriving, which means a day of delay in getting our community settled, which means delay in getting little John and others to join us. It leads my thoughts into a hole full of anxiety and worry. We made this commitment. I want to get there. I can only trust that God has perfect timing and a perfect plan.

Thank you for your prayers—I know you are praying for us. I am finding encouragement and peace through my readings even in the midst of this intense heat.

Friday, August 4

For I will pour water upon him that is thirsty, and floods upon the dry ground: I will pour my spirit upon thy seed, and my blessing upon thine offspring.
— Isaiah 44:3

Dear Jaqueline,

I am lonely for conversation with you. There is little time for conversation with my dear friends. The moms of little ones are in constant motion. Mary Brewster and I have tried many times to talk over morning tea, but our time is always cut short. Usually within a couple minutes she is up and chasing after one of the boys. Her drink becomes cold before she has a chance to sit back down. We laugh it off, but it is frustrating for both of us.

Mary Allerton's story is identical. Bartholomew is seven, Remember is five, and her little Mary is three. What a handful. Her three never stop moving, and while they are happy little children, as long as they are awake, they are up and moving around, and poor Mary rarely gets a minute to rest or sit down.

Agnes Tilley has her niece Humility. She just turned one and is the most playful of all our little ones. With bouncing blonde curls, she loves to practice her walking skills. Up and down the aisle she goes. It is most humorous. In spite of the heat and the lack of fresh air, these little ones are trying to make the most of this adventure.

For a few rare moments, Mary Allerton was able to join me on deck this afternoon for fresh air. Her little Mary was always a good playmate for little John, but even though our children played together many times, we've had few actual moments to converse.

She and Isaac have been married a couple years longer than William and me, and they already have three children, with one on the way. That makes my mind swirl, but she is well organized, efficient, and very fierce to protect all her children. We spent most of our time discussing the challenges of caring for a three-year-old, wanting them to be independent but at the same time dreading when they venture too far, and wanting them to stay little forever. She completely understands the full spectrum of my motherhood emotions in leaving a child behind; I feel now that I have a new comrade. She is struggling with the lack of fresh food on the ship, but I encouraged her to eat well for her strength as well as the baby's. I forgot that she had a miscarriage earlier this year. She says this baby will be her last. She is hopeful we are in homes by December so all will be good and ready for her delivery. I am hopeful for that too.

William is keenly aware of my need for female companionship, especially in light of being so far away from you. He will be pleased that I had a chance to visit with Mary.

Saturday, August 5

These things I have spoken unto you, that in me ye might have peace. In the world ye shall have tribulation: but be of good cheer; I have overcome the world.
— John 16:33

Dear Jaqueline,

At long last we set sail from Southampton early this morning. While the men watched from the upper deck, our little group of women and children gave a big cheer as we left the English Channel behind. A few of the older children led a cheerful parade down the middle aisle, banging pots and pans, shaking chains and coins and any noisemaker they could find. It is good to be on our way and worth celebrating with a few moments of good cheer.

But alas, no sooner do we celebrate leaving one frustration behind than we venture straight into the path of the next difficulty—the rolling waves of the western sea. There are hardly words for how massive these waves are. We crash head-on into each one, pounding and tossing our tiny ship. It's as if we are fighting our way out of a tumultuous water trap, clawing our way, inch by inch, in search of open flat waters. The motion is quite unwelcome, and many are sick. Occasionally we enter a section of calmer water where the sailing is smooth, and we begin to feel well again. Our spirits lift. I wonder how those on the *Mayflower* are faring.

Monday, August 7

For if thou altogether holdest thy peace at this time, then shall there en-
largement and deliverance arise to the Jews from another place; but thou and
thy father's house shall be destroyed: and who knoweth whether thou art come
to the kingdom for such a time as this?
— Esther 4:14

Dear Jaqueline,

It may seem silly to you, but this morning on deck I was reminded of
Mordecai's words to Queen Esther in Esther 4:14. She certainly found herself
in the most unusual of circumstances. I feel a bond with her for that reason.
But it's a silly comparison. Am I in a royal palace? Definitely not. Am I com-
paring this journey to the importance of her life-changing declaration? Of
course not. But her odd situation reminds me that for each of us, there are
life-changing moments when we are called to be courageous, to trust God,
to follow him into the complete unknown.

We definitely faced our share of difficulties in Leiden. And most definitely
we will face even more unknowns in this strange new land. And yet like Esther,
we overcome obstacles with patience and God's help. We do not allow small
inconveniences to discourage us. We do not allow small dissatisfactions to
drive us back to the safety of a homeland. Even though we have absolutely no
experience or skills to carve a settlement out of wilderness, we do not let that
stop us. We are going where God leads, to do whatever he is calling us to do.
If that's to create a village where we can worship as we intend or if that's to be
a stepping-stone in some future sense of God's plan, so be it.

On one hand, I don't see that we have the same sense of immediate danger as Esther faced in being put to death for approaching the king. However,
it strikes me that here I am, out in the middle of a vast ocean, and I have completely put my life at risk to be able to worship God as I see proper. I have
chosen to be obedient even if it leads to death. I have asked questions late
into the midnight hours, as I know Esther must have, but in the end I am as
confident as she was of God's goodness and grace and have chosen to go forward, asking no questions, being willing to be of extreme service to the King
and completely trusting my life in his hands. Was she brave or crazy or both?
Either way she took her place in God's story, and I pray that this journey and
our obedience will bring him as much delight as Esther's did.

Yes, my story is different from Esther's, but it is similar in many ways. I am thankful for those who recorded her story, as it has given me a new sense of courage today.

Thursday, August 10

Till we all come in the unity of the faith, and of the knowledge of the Son of God, unto a perfect man, unto the measure of the stature of the fulness of Christ.
— Ephesians 4:13

Dear Jaqueline,

All I can say is that it has been a long day, and I desperately need sleep. Most of the families are resting before our evening meal. It's quiet here below, but for some reason sleep won't come for me. I know there is a long journey ahead, and probably the best thing I can do is sleep. I'm tired and mentally exhausted, but I lie here wide-awake and thinking of nothing in particular. I try to picture pleasant things: little John running through the backyard, his smile, your face. I try to picture each of you, wondering what you and Momma are doing this afternoon, hoping that will relax my thoughts. I know sleep will eventually come but will probably not last long. That is the pattern of these days.

Last night when this same thing happened, I focused on a passage of scripture— Ephesians 4:13. I spent a long time pondering what it meant, and it made me realize that my prayers should not focus so narrowly on my own spiritual development. This verse calls us to broaden our prayers so that we *all* come to know God better. There is no doubt that I personally need to daily grow closer to God, but this verse is God's call to the entire community of believers, not just me but all individuals and families; it alters the perspective of my prayers. I will pray that the entire body of Christ will be built up. Does that make sense to you?

Anyway, I learned that focusing my thoughts on one scripture brought a sense of calmness, and I was eventually able to fall asleep. I pray that sense of calmness will return today.

Sunday, August 13

But the Comforter, which is the Holy Ghost, whom the Father will send in my name, he shall teach you all things, and bring all things to your remembrance, whatsoever I have said unto you.
— John 14:26

Dear Jaqueline,

A major setback. It's been only eight days since we left Southampton, but they discovered another leak in the *Speedwell*. We are now in port at Dartmouth.

Frustration abounds. It becomes more and more of a battle to keep this mission going. Each step backward seems a direct attempt by Satan to throw us off course, weaken us, discourage us, deter us from going on.

Elder Brewster continues to encourage us with reminders of God's presence here with us. I am beginning to see God's wisdom in selecting him as the spiritual leader of our group. He has a unique quality of calmness during the chaos and a special gift of discerning the next steps. Yesterday, for example, when the crew reported this most recent concern, Elder Brewster addressed our group in a factual tone. He outlined all the steps they would take in repair. He kept the group appeased while maintaining order. He answered all the questions regarding supplies and timing and expense and treated every question respectfully. Some families are poised and ready to spin into a panic. Elder Brewster's gift for keeping us focused on seeing Jesus as our Provider, our Guide, and our Victor is more than a blessing.

Cushman quickly assembled a team of workers, so I pray repairs do not take too long. At least the seaport is busy and fascinating. William and I spent half of the day on the upper deck, watching ships arrive and depart: small ships, large-masted ships, ships of all shapes and sizes. I wish little John were here, to share this brief experience, this small snippet of the journey with us. It would give him a new appreciation for our travels.

Thursday, August 17

Why art thou cast down, O my soul? and why art thou disquieted within me? hope thou in God: for I shall yet praise him, who is the health of my countenance, and my God.
— Psalm 42:11

My dear sister,

Panic has officially set in, and it is not a pretty sight. The *Speedwell* is repaired, and we are ready to leave Dartmouth, but now the winds are not cooperating. Another delay; we sit and sit, wasting days of precious time.

Throughout the morning you could visually see the tension mounting. Mothers snapped at children. Children tried desperately to be quiet so as not to disturb the men. William, Edward, and several others paced back and forth in the middle aisle, wringing their hands, occasionally grunting a phrase or two, hoping to release some of the frustration. John Alden, the cooper who joined us at Southampton, did a thorough check of our barrels and announced that our provisions are dwindling quickly and will likely be half-gone before we reach America. That was not welcome news.[10]

Martin, who is now governor of our *Speedwell*, commanded all passengers (the men too) to stay aboard the ship. When Elder Brewster brought that news to us down below, I gave William one of my "I don't like the sound of this" looks. It truly puzzled me. Is Martin concerned that we would get lost in the unfamiliar town of Dartmouth? Is he worried that we will run away? And what if we did? William whispered to me that he is not sure what gives Martin any right to control the whereabouts of every person on our ship, but I suppose we will be obedient. Some of our passengers are upset by today's happenings and started murmurs of abandoning the journey. Others are trying to make light of the situation, saying Martin is completely irrational. I don't really have any desire to get off the ship or explore Dartmouth. All I can hope is that the winds will soon shift, and we will be on our way.

Wednesday, August 23

How excellent is thy lovingkindness, O God! therefore the children of men put their trust under the shadow of thy wings.

They shall be abundantly satisfied with the fatness of thy house; and thou shalt make them drink of the river of thy pleasures.

— Psalm 36:7–8

Jaqueline,

This morning our crew was attentive, and with the noticeable shift in wind we set sail from Dartmouth. Praise God! It was a tricky departure because many ships in port were taking advantage of the prime winds. We made it several miles past the tip of England before—you guessed it—they discovered *another* leak.

Unfortunately, this one appears to be more serious than the others. All is in a bit of an uproar. Tempers are flaring. Accusations are flying. Elder Brewster is extremely concerned. He mentioned it may be time to give up the *Speedwell*, but those are alarming words coming from our fearless leader, the one who usually keeps us focused on the task at hand. One look at William, however, tells me all I need to know. He is confident; he is stable; he immediately focuses on the problem at hand without thinking too far ahead. True, we don't know what this setback will lead to, but we will trust that God is leading us and trust that the outcome will be good. It's times like this when William's steadiness keeps me anchored.

Monday, August 28

While we look not at the things which are seen, but at the things which are not seen: for the things which are seen are temporal; but the things which are not seen are eternal.
— 2 Corinthians 4:18

Dear Jaqueline,

We put in at Plymouth on the west coast of England this morning, another amazing seaport. After meeting with the crew and all the men, Elder Brewster gathered our group to outline the options. It is time to give up the *Speedwell*, and each family will now have a choice to make. This is a great loss for our community. The ship cost us considerable money and time in the repairs of the last few weeks.[11]

However, there is room aboard the *Mayflower*, and Elder Brewster has already met with Master Jones. All on board the *Mayflower* are willing to make room for the *Speedwell* passengers, in spite of the fact that it will be extremely crowded. Some *Speedwell* passengers are still troubled by the consistent and discouraging delays of the journey so far. Some see this as God's warning and direct guidance to abandon, find a way back to Leiden, and make the journey next spring.

William is convinced, although not sharing it widely, that Master Reynolds is a rascal and some of his crew may have created these leaks and delays on purpose. Could that even be possible? Would men be so dreading this journey to go to that extreme? William speculates they purposefully overmasted the *Speedwell*, giving her masts that were too tall or too heavy for a ship her size. It doesn't make sense to me, but I do know that fear will lead a man down many paths. If that is the case with Master Reynolds and his crew, then I wish them good riddance. Even though I was initially impressed with their mannerisms and charm, it is clear to see that they have abandoned all responsibility. In fact, Master Reynolds is nowhere to be found at the moment.[12]

Tuesday, August 29

And thine ears shall hear a word behind thee, saying, This is the way, walk ye in it, when ye turn to the right hand, and when ye turn to the left.
— Isaiah 30:21

My dear Jaqueline,

In the late hours of last night, William asked that we pray about our decision. I was a bit surprised, as we've never once thought of abandoning the initial call, but William felt it important to once again seek God for direction. Abandoning now would mean returning to Leiden for the winter and making the journey in the spring with the others.

There are a thousand logical reasons to return home, but will God's work be done if we return home instead of staying on board? Of course, there have been challenges, worries, and tears. But there hasn't been one day of looking back with regret. We have our eyes set on America. But this choice is before us, so we will take time and pray for God to confirm the way.

It's almost a bit comical that God even provides this type of opportunity for reexamination. It's as if God wants us to know, beyond a shadow of doubt, where he wants us to be and what he wants us to do. Is this his way of leading us into a deeper level of trust? His way of molding and shaping us to be all that he wants us to be? Or is this truly his way of telling us that the path ahead will be too difficult, too stressful, and too dangerous and that we must return home? Is this his way of testing us, saying, "I see now that you've trusted me to come this far. That is all I wanted; you can return home now and wait for the next direction." Is this his way of telling us once again, "This is the path I want you on; this *is* the plan"? It is so hard to know.

We pray, and there is absolute silence. I trust that silence; it brings absolute peace. We have no inclination to change course, no leading to change direction, no strong sense that we are to get off this boat and say goodbye to the others. The desire to continue on this adventure remains strong for both William and me. We know there will be struggles. We know this journey will likely test us to the very core of our faith. God makes it clear that we should stay the course. He has been faithful to provide each step of the way so far. God willing, we will continue to grow strong in our faith and in our resolve to serve. In spite of uncertainties that creep in from many angles, including diminishing food supplies, leaving the *Speedwell* behind, and having a very late traveling season, we remain entirely submissive to the will of God. We completely surrender to what we've been created to accomplish. Our purpose in the journey has not diminished. We will stay, and God's mighty hand goes before us.

Wednesday, August 30

And if it seem evil unto you to serve the Lord, choose you this day whom ye will serve; whether the gods which your fathers served that were on the other side of the flood, or the gods of the Amorites, in whose land ye dwell: but as for me and my house, we will serve the Lord.
— Joshua 24:15

Jaqueline,

Some entire families have decided to return home, about twenty from our congregation in total. It is heartbreaking. They will find a way back to Leiden. I pray they don't regret their decision, but I can honestly say I am thrilled that Cushman is among them.

While Cushman has been a great help to our group, assisting Carver with our work agreements in Virginia, I've continued to have the feeling that he has been overwhelmed by some of the challenges given to him in that role.[13] Granted, I can imagine that any man taking on that responsibility for our congregation would have a great burden of worry, but he has been complaining incessantly about heart problems since we left Southampton. He will be better off to make the journey next spring. I am thankful as well that his good friends William Ring and Thomas Blossom have chosen to stay behind as well.[14] William and I agree that we will be better off without having to listen to their negative thoughts and attitudes.

With Cushman leaving, Martin has agreed to step down, and we will all be governed by Carver, who has been assigned governor of the *Mayflower*. That is, of course, a wonderful benefit to know that we will be under the authority of Carver. His strong negotiation skills and highly approachable nature make him a perfect choice to oversee those of us from Leiden as well as all the Londoners already aboard the *Mayflower*.

William announced we will take a spot on the *Mayflower*, and there was visible relief all around. The Brewsters will continue on, as will the Allertons, Dr. Fuller, and the Winslows. I'm pleased that Uncle William and Aunt Susanna will continue as well. The size of our Leiden group is reduced, but it is a good, strong group of individuals. And I think, now having had a chance to walk away and yet choosing clearly to commit again, we are united in our purpose, wherever it leads.

I am also very pleased that the Tinkers have decided to stay the course.

Jane Tinker is one of the most positive women in our group, and the loss of even one personality like hers would be difficult for our women. She is one of those with a rare gift to be able to relate to almost every individual. She is approachable and pleasant. I don't think I've ever seen her angry or upset with anyone, especially her son. She exemplifies encouragement, and Lord knows we need all of that we can get.

Perhaps this has been God's intention all along—to send us on one ship together. As I write, provisions are being transferred from the *Speedwell* to the *Mayflower*. It's time to settle into an even smaller space.

Friday, September 1

But the fruit of the Spirit is love, joy, peace, longsuffering, gentleness,
goodness, faith,
   Meekness, temperance: against such there is no law.
   — Galatians 5:22–23

Dear Jaqueline,

I marvel at some of these women. Agnes Tilley, for example. She and Edward have no children of their own, but she has her hands full with bringing both her sister's son Henry and her brother's baby Humility. But she takes it all in stride.

Agnes tells us it was Edward's decision, not hers, to bring both children. Last winter her sister approached them about Henry, who had just turned sixteen. Edward insisted that bringing him on the voyage would provide an incredible future for the lad. Then last spring when her brother Robert lost his wife shortly after childbirth, Edward again insisted they bring the baby girl. Agnes touts that Edward has an amazingly kind heart, but more importantly he feels strongly about family loyalty whether it's an inconvenience or not. (This trait reminds me of you, by the way.) He made the decision because it was the right thing to do. Fortunately, Humility is healthy and happy. Her tight, curly ringlets bounce with every move, this way and that. She doesn't know a stranger and cries little; no one seems to mind when she crawls right into an open family space. Agnes is ever watchful of her but has expressed many times an appreciation of our community approach to family care.

Agnes is also fortunate to have her sister-in-law Joan bunking to her left. Even though they're not blood relatives, you'd never know it. Joan's husband, John, is brother to Edward. Their daughter, Elizabeth, is thirteen and tends to Humility as if she were her own sister. Their family bonds are strong. Henry, Elizabeth, and Humility, though cousins from three different families, sit together and eat together, and when they venture to the upper deck, there is Humility in between the two older ones, holding each of their hands. Maybe it's their personal mission to see the little girl safely to America.

In the last couple days, I've watched as Desire Minter joins their threesome. Desire and Elizabeth are close in age, if not the same. I poke William every time I see them huddle together. Desire has not known a real family. Her father died when she was nine, and before her mother remarried, Desire was passed from caretaker to caretaker. Now as a servant appointed to the Carvers, she is getting a fresh, new start.

Was it providence that the Carvers would bunk right next to the Tilleys? Indeed. It's almost as if you can see how God is molding and shaping the life of each individual on this journey. It's like we are each a colored thread being woven into a beautiful tapestry that will provide warmth and security for the community in the New World. I wonder what color my thread is.

Saturday, September 2

*For whosoever shall give you a cup of water to drink in my name, because
ye belong to Christ, verily I say unto you, he shall not lose his reward.*
— Mark 9:41

Dear Jaqueline,

This morning my thoughts and prayers are for Bridget Robinson. Mary
Brewster mentioned her name at morning meal, and I haven't been able to
stop thinking about her since. I pray that she is getting along well with the
pregnancy. I pray that the older Brewster children that stayed behind are
being a help to her. I miss her so and long for her company and the way she
makes us all laugh. If anyone could, she would be the one to find humor as
we squeeze aboard the *Mayflower*.

I am anxious for news of her family's day-to-day details. Mary, John, and
Isaac—are they getting along well with lessons? How are Mercy and Fear? If
they were here, they would race on the deck or set up an obstacle course,
anything to relieve the misery of waiting for a fair wind. They have all been
an integral part of my daily routine for so many years that I'm finding it a bit
painful now without them.

I laugh to myself thinking of Bridget in that messy household full of
happy children. She would laugh at us right now trying to keep everything
so tidy and neat. It's comical—we are a group of messy people, and I mean
that both literally and figuratively. She is always at her best with messy people,
teaching them how to walk with Jesus. She is the best I know at living out
what she believes. She always takes time to tell a story that would make us
laugh till our sides hurt. Her problems are never more important than taking
out time to love a person, any person. She honors others above herself. She
is joyful in the midst of chaos. She is gracious and sensitive to the needs of
others around her. She truly lives out Romans 12 and practices hospitality. I
need to be more like her.

I agree with William that all things happen for a reason, but I continue
to be puzzled at Pastor's decision to stay behind. I understand that with six
children and one expected, they had sufficient reason to consider all options.
But are they better off now staying behind, or do they regret their decision
from the moment our ship pulled away? Thinking back, I wonder how many
were influenced by them. I don't want to criticize. I am more than anxious

for their company and will miss them daily until they join us. Won't Pastor be surprised when he learns how small a group we've become? I wonder if those who've turned back will return to Leiden or stay in England. My questions are pointless, the result of idle time here, waiting, waiting. . .

Monday, September 4

Blessed are the meek: for they shall inherit the earth.
— Matthew 5:5

Dear Jaqueline,

There's not been a waking moment yet when I don't think of you and little John. Literally you are my first thoughts each morning. I wonder what you are doing. I think about how delightful our agenda for the day would be if it included a game of chase around the yard.

After the morning meal, I stretch my legs on deck, and my mind wanders back to you. The constant activity of this harbor reminds me of little John's endless supply of energy and playfulness, from sunup to sundown. I wonder if you are already entering the days of late summer when leaves begin to yellow. I wonder if the neighborhood barn swallows have left their nests to migrate south. It occurs to me that I have missed an entire month of summer and now likely will miss the entire stretch of summer changing to fall.

I enjoy the buzz of activity on deck, but today my private thoughts were interrupted by Peter Browne and the dogs. One is a giant mastiff, as gentle and loving as they come but full of brute strength. The dog could knock me over if I wasn't paying attention. The other is a spaniel, lovable, alert, and full of spunk. The dogs are owned by John Goodman, and William says they are well-known locally for their expert retrieving skills. Both dogs will be a tremendous help once we are settled and the hunting excursions begin, but Browne is quite taken with them. Browne is from Dorking and travels as apprentice to the Mullins family. The Mullinses bunk next to Goodman, so that has all worked out nicely. Both Browne and the Mullins children—Priscilla and Joseph—seem to have a true love for animals. I see them frequently on deck together, taking the dogs on a lead or talking to the chickens and rabbits.

It's funny to me how God sometimes places these people in my life, for no other reason than to pray for them. I am reminded of some of the people from Leiden that I'd run into over and over again, on the street, in the shop. Some people caught my eye for some reason. The one man who worked for the jeweler—I never knew his name, but day after day he walked the same path and seemed so burdened with life. The one woman I met in the park. She was so energetic and full of life. She had young children too, so when I ran into her at the market, I immediately recognized her as the lady from the park. After that I saw her several places around our area. And there was the man in the shoe shop. And the young man with the disability of some type. I'd see these faces in places all over town—familiar to me because I'd see them again and again, yet completely unknown. We never spoke. Then one day it dawned on me that if God brought them into my life over and over again, perhaps it was because they needed a prayer or two.

Anyway, back to the Mullins family. William and Alice Mullins are from Dorking. Mullins is a shoemaker and quite a successful one at that. He made quite a large investment in our company before our send-off from Southampton, but my William says he was also involved in some sort of religious controversy, which may be the reason they have joined us. Regardless, they are a kindhearted, jovial group, and I hope to get better acquainted with them.[15]

Their children, Priscilla and Joseph, have captured my attention and now my daily prayers too. Joseph seems well-adjusted and is quickly making friends. Perhaps it's easier for the younger ones. I know for Wrestling and Love, this is one great big incredible adventure. Priscilla on the other hand must be close to seventeen or eighteen, which seems to be the defining age when one could have stayed behind or come along, depending on the parents' insistence and the child's independence. Many of the older children in Leiden chose to stay behind, planning to come with the rest of the congregation next year. Priscilla seems to have the independence of one who could have chosen to stay behind. She seems a bit unhappy, so I speculate that it wasn't her choice to come along. Her family seems respectful of one another. There doesn't seem to be any argument among them, so it's hard to imagine that the parents forced her to come along. She may be fine about being here, but she rarely interacts with anyone outside her family, except for Peter Browne. She rarely attends our community meetings. She sometimes attends the lessons but is older than most of the school-age children and younger than the adults. I guess that's why my heart goes out to her. She doesn't seem to fit anywhere and desperately needs a friend.

Priscilla is both beautiful and strong. I've seen her help her mother with organization and meals. She is obedient and works hard. She often wears her hair braided down one side and then forward over her shoulder. She carries herself in a confident manner and is most adoring to her mother and father and brother. But she is quiet, spends her time reading, and often looks deep in thought. I wonder if she has many friends back home.

Without even knowing Priscilla at all, I am praying for her. Praying that she finds her place. Praying that our God, who knows every thought she is thinking, will provide for her every need. Praying that God grants her the courage and confidence she will need to live with this group of strangers in our new community. Praying she will find a friend to make her journey more enjoyable, someone who enjoys the same activities, someone who will lift her spirits, someone she can confide in and laugh with.

I'd invite her to join the ladies' discussion times, but I doubt that would be appealing. She might feel out of place among a group of non-stop jabbering women. I pray God will help her with her responsibilities, keep her strong and healthy. I pray that God will continue to draw her to know him better and grow her faith and trust in him alone, continuing to teach her about grace and mercy and love. After all it's only with God that one will find true contentment and peace. It's only through God that one finds the freedom to become oneself. I hope to get to know more about her and will be anxious to report back to you how we see God working in her life.

Wednesday, September 6

If the Son therefore shall make you free, ye shall be free indeed.
— John 8:36

Greetings Jaqueline,

"A prosperous wind," William proclaimed out loud from the railing today, and I fully agreed. As we set sail from Plymouth this morning, the wind smelled of hope and freedom. I breathed in the deepest breath I possibly could, inhaling the full smells of sea, salt, and sand. It was the type of breeze that went all the way into the full depth of my lungs like the fair breeze that completely fills the ship's sail. The only possible response was a deep exhale of sigh and release. We quickly went to full sail, and the excitement of the crew was contagious. Master Jones exclaimed, "We are on our way!" and all on deck laughed in hearty agreement. Having turned back twice already, maybe a more practical exclamation would have been "now or never!"

It is late in the season, but there is warmth in the air and a gentle wind, so all I needed was my light cape on deck. Something felt different about today's departure, as if we were truly now fully committed, no going back. A deep sense of peace washed over me. Maybe it's because we are now more practiced at departures from the mainland. We know more of what to expect at sea, as if the first few launches were for practice. Now we are readied and prepared. This entire group—men, women, children, crew—all are committed and understand the intensity of this obligation. We are fully settled in, and there is no turning back, not at this time of year. We are already over a month into the supplies and six weeks later into the sailing season. If God intends us to make it, then the timing of the seasons and the amount of food we have doesn't matter. This journey is in his hands, and we are holding securely to our trust of that plan.

Pastor Robinson often spoke of being pilgrims on our journey to making heaven our home. Today, it feels like we are pilgrims in a different sense of the word, trying to find our new home in the New World—a home where we shall at last raise our families without fear of dishonoring God, without fear of worshipping the way we know we should, without fear of the King, without fear of prison. Although I suppose if the King wants to change his mind, he could send forces a thousand miles across the ocean to keep us in line. He was wise in promising that if we remain respectful in our mentions of his name, he will let us worship as we please. I wonder whether he wanted to be rid of us or whether God softened his heart.

William and I stayed on deck most of the morning. It was thrilling to watch the land disappear behind us and the sea to the west grow large. Our ship kept a steady pace of three or four knots, as if she were as excited as we are to finally be underway. Already we saw true wonders along the way. Seagulls became fewer and fewer as we moved into the deep. Pelicans entertained us as they dove for food, and a small school of porpoises swam off to the north. They traveled alongside our ship for a good way, as if they were a committee sent to see us off and cheer us on the way.

Little John would love this part of the journey, with the abundance of fish; all the stories we read about the ocean and its fish are true. I am anxious for him to see this. Some of these fish are two or three yards long. William tries to sketch them, but he is not good at drawing. In the middle of the afternoon, William called me to the deck. He spotted an odd fish floating by the ship's side. It was about a yard in length and completely round. Master Jones called it a sunfish, but William looked it up tonight and believes it was a large jellyfish. It first appeared like a large bubble above the water. Little John would be fascinated.

Again, my thoughts shift to those who chose to stay behind. Why do you suppose those specific ones were not to come with us at this time? God never sends us where he can't provide for us. Should we assume that God knows the trouble they would have faced ahead and either knows they were not up to the task or knows that they are needed instead to stay behind for a different family need or reason? I am trusting in God's infinite wisdom and will be curious to see what becomes of those families, to see where God leads them or what purpose they are called to. I look back at it now and am simply amazed how God maneuvered those circumstances.

Along that same line of thought, I can't get over the fact that God, in his infinite wisdom, has trimmed us down to one ship. We are crowded, but I pinch myself to think that William and I are on the *Mayflower*. Here I thought we would make the full journey on the *Speedwell* and was almost envious of those who would make the journey on a grand ship as the *Mayflower*. Now God has seen fit to make this my ship as well. Of course, I feel a special tie because it contains our family name. I know Momma will be so pleased when she gets word that we transferred to the *Mayflower*—one of her favorite spring flowers. I can picture even now those delicate tiny flowers that covered the back fields of our Cambridgeshire farm every spring. Such is the fresh promise of the *Mayflower*. She is a beautiful and sturdy ship, seaworthy for sure, and bears her name proudly. Her deck is strong, and most important, she doesn't leak!

Friday, September 8

I will lift up mine eyes unto the hills, from whence cometh my help.
My help cometh from the Lord, which made heaven and earth.
— Psalm 121:1–2

Dear Jaqueline,

Our prosperous wind continues, as does our pace, but many are now afflicted with seasickness. They don't like the fresh air on the upper deck, but I am establishing a routine to climb the ladder both early in the morning and late into the afternoon. Watching the sun on the water and the clouds floating gently above the horizon gives me the encouragement I need for making it through the day in the lower deck. While God's presence is always with me, up on deck I feel his peace and strength to the point of overflowing. It's like filling up my teacup and drinking in as much of his light and goodness as I possibly can.

I've discovered a small niche where I can stand out of the way of the crew. The view from my spot is quite amazing, unlike anything I've ever experienced before, and I find it hard to describe. There's nothing, and I mean nothing, but water, sky, and clouds in every direction I look. And as far as my eyes can see, we are the only ones in this section of the world. Quite an odd feeling—this view of a huge expanse of space and not another ship, not another person in sight. No trees, no buildings, no grass, no fields. Nothing but water and sky. For some it might stir a lonely feeling. For me it brings a complete sense of calm and purpose. It is an odd sensation that we've left thousands upon thousands of people behind and are truly now a community of a hundred.

Occasionally I have seen a ship's sail far, far in the distance, but none have threatened or even have the appearance of threatening so far. We are experiencing God's grace in that matter.

And this water, Jaqueline... it's different. It's not like the easygoing water we're used to seeing in the canal, with gurgles and streams running swiftly over rocks. It's nothing compared to the calm blue water in the Channel on those days when we'd take a picnic to watch the boats and soak in the sun. This water is big and powerful, like none I've ever seen before. Waves sometimes swell so high and dip our ship so low that I think they could swallow our ship whole, sails and all, in one huge gulp. This water is a dark, dark blue like my warm navy blanket, but it is cold and dark, very cold. Master Jones tells me the dark, dark color means the water is very deep, so deep that no light can even reach the floor of the ocean. To some of our passengers, this water brings a complete sense of insecurity; they see the ship as a tiny, minuscule object in an immense body of water, watching the water rush up and along the sides of the ship, over and over again. For me it's helpful to keep my eyes focused on what's above the water instead of imagining what might be below.

I easily become entranced watching the clouds overhead. Sometimes they are wispy and light. Sometimes they form tiny puffs or become billowy and full. They are never the same from moment to moment, a continuous metamorphosis from one shape into another. I like to think of the clouds as God's footprints as he walks about in the heavens. It puts him in the right perspective for me. On deck I am so filled with an awareness of the divine Creator's presence. I grow more confident day after day that he is watching over us, guiding us knot by knot to the exact place he has selected for setting up our community.

It's one thing to trust that we are moving forward at a good pace, but there are no landmarks to give one the sense that we are moving from one point to another. Without any nautical instruments, it can seem as though we are not moving at all. An odd sensation indeed. It sometimes gives me the sense of being lost. It is completely unsettling to some, so much so that they won't come up on deck. My dearest Mary Brewster refuses to visit the upper deck for very long because it makes her queasy to watch the water that surrounds us.

William Butten doesn't like it either. He is servant to Dr. Fuller and looks to be a young teen. I found him this morning clearly distraught and asked what was bothering him. He looked around cautiously to make sure no one could hear, then whispered he was afraid of the water. He never learned to swim, and the thought of falling overboard is terrifying. It haunts him morning and night. He is fearful of the water's chill and all the unknowns that swim under the surface. This fear is on top of still being nauseated almost every day from seasickness.

I didn't find many words to comfort him. But I did tell him what you always taught me—when you're afraid, find someone to talk to. Talk about anything to get your mind off of the fear. So, we talked. About his family, about his dreams. His father died when he was young, and his mother was unable to provide for him financially. You'd think he would be full of despair, but this young boy is full of life. He talked about his favorite color, blue—the robin's-egg blue of a warm spring sky. He talked about his friends and some of their adventures. He shared how Dr. Fuller has been so kind and generous to him, teaching him everything he possibly can. He told me some funny jokes that I wasn't even sure I understood, but it was so enjoyable to see him animated that it made me laugh out loud, not laughing at him but truly laughing with him. Once I got him talking, he rambled on and on and on and completely forgot, or almost completely forgot, about his fear. Laughter is good medicine.

I also shared with him the other thing you taught me, which is when you're fearful or worried or overwhelmed by everything around you, it's time to lift your eyes to the heavens. It always seems to help my nausea to get my eyes and my thoughts focused on anything other than the water. There's something calming in watching the clouds drift from west to east. I picture them floating all the way east to your house and wonder how many times they will change shape between here and there. Or maybe they will cycle through a pattern of changes, and by the time they are directly over your house, they are the exact same shape as what I am seeing above me now. These are the thoughts that calm me down, the thoughts that bring a return of peace and deep breathing to my once nerve-racked, chaotic sense of despair.

Later this afternoon Butten tapped me on the elbow and said "thank you." It was good to share those valuable lessons. And now I have a new friend.

Sunday, September 10

He telleth the number of the stars; he calleth them all by their names.
— Psalm 147:4

Dear Jaqueline,

This morning we passed the point of our turnaround, literally the point where the *Speedwell* turned around for the second time. Some of us gave salute at the passing point to honor the ship that carried us for thirty-three days.

Waves are larger and stronger now. Many are not feeling good at all, including me. I fell asleep easily last night but woke up early, as there is little rest from the queasiness at night. Sleepless nights do not make for productive days, so I excused myself from afternoon services for a nap. Here I rest, and there are three things I am most grateful for today that I must make note of.

First, I am grateful to be completely free of the city, crowds, politics, danger of prison, and fear of someone knocking on our door. It took me a few days to realize that we are finally free from those fears, those anxieties we lived with for a long time. It will take me a while to get used to not always looking over my shoulder in suspicion. Such freedom accompanies us on this journey.

Second, I am thankful for the amazing quiet. I don't remember anything quite like it before. The wind whooshes in the canvas sails. The waves splash repetitively against the hull. A baby cries now and then. Friends rustle in the middle of afternoon chores. Crewmen shout continually on deck from bow to stern. But it's quiet. No city sounds, no wind blowing in the trees, no dogs barking, no busyness.

Those who stayed behind at Plymouth may never know this amazing sense of quiet. It's a lost opportunity for them, I'm afraid. I still don't understand what happened to their courage. I am still not sure I completely understand how they had a sudden change of heart, how their excitement turned so quickly to discouragement. I'm too tired to be critical of their choice. I pray they find peace with their decision. As for me, in this broad expanse of quiet, I find more stability than on any solid ground we've been on since moving to Leiden. Isn't that funny? More peace out in the middle of nowhere than on any shore we've been on yet.

And one more thing I am so grateful for today is God opening my eyes to recognize his perfect timing for this journey. Could we have made this trip one hundred years ago? Absolutely not; no vessel was equipped to take this large of a group as far as we're going. Could we have received the blessing of any other king, a blessing that would allow us to work and set up a community of faith? Absolutely not; I am so thankful for King James and his willingness to let us go. On one hand, there's a feeling that we've escaped, and yet no one's pursuing us; no one's chasing us. Maybe the King is glad to be rid of us, but I marvel how all the pieces fell into place to bring us here—to the middle of nowhere.

I hope little John is not keeping you up all hours of the night. I know how exhausting that can be. My love and continued thanks and prayers for all you do.

Tuesday, September 12

I will both lay me down in peace, and sleep: for thou, Lord, only makest me dwell in safety.
– Psalm 4:8

Jaqueline,

On cloudy nights it seems to take longer for our families to settle down. Some of the little ones are uncomfortable on such nights, but they finally find sleep as the lower deck fills with the darkest dark I've known.

The air is dark, the water outside is dark and deep, and with no stars or moon shining, it becomes difficult to see anything around me at all. And this darkness, Jaqueline. . . it's different—I don't mean that it's a hellish blackness or a darkness accompanied by despair or torture or imprisonment. While it hints at the many things unknown, there is no fear in this dark. It's like a blank page in a new book, mysterious yet exciting, a new chapter in our lives, waiting to be written. It is air and space we have not yet breathed before. Yes, it indicates that we are headed into uncharted territory. It will be our witness on the long journey ahead. My mind fills with visions of what the land will look like, of whom we will encounter.

I've learned the layout of the deck well by now. Brewsters are to my right, Allertons are to my left. I recognize their movements and shifts, their whispered voices. In the daylight I'd liken this space to more of a crawl space. People and clothing, chests and casks, furniture and bedding, all overflow and spill into the aisles. But in the dark of night, our deck is almost airless.

Oddly enough the little amount of air is full of trust—I trust so many of these passengers and crew by now. Those from Leiden are a true demonstration of God's drawing power. We are continually reminded of his hand at work in our lives by how our glorious Savior brought this particular group of persons together and gifted us with unity. And in spite of the unknowns, we are forming a strong bond with many of the Londoners, developing common goals and a desire to help one another. In that sense, this darkness, this journey, is teaching us to cooperate with one another, strangers included, for our common goals. Instead of fear and mistrust, the darkness speaks of courage and strength, of the ability to lean on your neighbor for assistance, of a growing love for one another, of hope and excitement that we are facing the unknown not by ourselves but with a group of common pilgrims.

I have a new awareness of God's presence, here in this darkest of dark places on these darkest of dark nights. I almost laugh out loud at the circumstances. I am amazed at the comfort our good Shepherd provides to this handful of families, even in this small way of filling darkness with his light and peace so we can get needed sleep. How well he knows us and all our needs.

Thursday, September 14

This is my commandment, That ye love one another, as I have loved you. Greater love hath no man than this, that a man lay down his life for his friends.
— John 15:12–13

Dear Jaqueline,

I don't want to complain. If I start down the path of complaining, I might not be able to stop, and I certainly can't afford to get into that mindset. However, we have a family of four that joined us in Southampton that is quite unbelievable. The Billingtons: mother, father, and two teenage boys. I'm guessing they are thirteen and fifteen, but I don't have much experience in guessing ages. The entire group appears to be nothing but trouble. I can sum it up for you by saying that the Billingtons would have lived on the east end of town.

Why in heaven's name God thought it was a good idea for their family to join our company is beyond me. And why on earth they even *wanted* to join our voyage is puzzling. They have no business going to the remote wilderness, let alone uniting with our group. Not a whit of sense between the lot of them. I speculate Billington must be in some sort of trouble with the law and is using the *Mayflower* as his only source of escape. I can't imagine why else they are here. They boarded with few provisions, so I even wonder if someone paid them to leave town quickly.

To provide you with a visual, I would compare Mr. B to the scoundrel we used to avoid on the corner of Derby Street. Do you remember him—the one known for picking pockets? Mr. B is tall, sloppy, loudmouthed, and profane all day long. He smells of whiskey most times and has even been seen walking the public aisle in his nightclothes and nightcap. Elder Brewster has had several conversations with him, hoping he would at least control his tongue around the women and children, but to no avail yet.

Add Mrs. B to the picture, and what a perfect pair; she is unkempt, loud, and almost as profane as Mr. B. She tries to rule the boys, but we often hear spankings, yelling, and arguing. My eyes go wide when I hear the boys argue back with Mrs. B and her attempts to discipline. Their insults are completely improper, yet neither parent seems to have any control over the two. Both boys are extremely disrespectful and disobedient. They run rampant throughout the entire ship. It's a wonder the crew hasn't knuckled one of them yet, but I won't be surprised when it happens. They are a family in constant motion, more like a whirlwind. Thankfully they have taken space at the end of our long aisle, so I have little interaction with them.

Except yesterday—Mr. B approached me in the food line and asked if I knew anything about the clump of dirt that appeared in his soup. I was quite speechless about the entire encounter. Why would I have anything to do with dirt in his soup? There is dirt everywhere you look around here. Is it any wonder that dirt does not appear in every bowl of soup we serve? I had no words. Thankfully Aunt Susanna was working beside me in the food line and quickly rose to my defense. With the biggest smile she apologized and handed him a fresh bowl of soup. I could have been most offended by his near accusation, but it's pointless, and I had to let it go.

I am determined to build bridges instead of walls with the Billingtons and all the other strangers. Aunt Susanna thinks they are an odd bunch and says we should keep our distance. Uncle William says there is some good in all people, but I will have to dig deep to find it here.

Friday, September 15

Be not forgetful to entertain strangers: for thereby some have entertained angels unawares.
— Hebrews 13:2

Dear Jaqueline,

I finally got a chance to talk to Priscilla Mullins. She is unbelievably sweet. We happened to sit down next to each other at the evening meal. At first, I thought, "Oh no, she'll soon wish she was sitting by someone her own age, and we won't have much to talk about." But I was most wrong.

I introduced myself, and of course she knew who I was, but how can you even begin a conversation without a proper introduction? I can't even remember the first question she asked, but when I answered, I noticed how intently she listened, as if she were actually interested. The experience was so different from that of talking to mothers, who are often busy making sure their own children behave and eat well. It was fascinating. After a few minutes of talking and laughing and getting to know Priscilla, I felt as if I'd know her a long time.

Knowing her love for animals, I told her all about the pets we used to have. She laughed at my stories of Brigadier. I told her about the afternoon Brigadier escaped from the house while you had the back door open. You remember this, right? I can still picture us running down the road, chasing after that little dog, yelling at him to stop, which only seemed to make him run faster. I'm not exactly sure how we ever caught him, but she thought that was so funny.

She talked about her love for animals and all the creatures of the ocean. She was originally hoping to go to university to study science. She had only heard of one other woman ever going to a university, and her older brother and sister thought she had the potential to make her case to a university. Instead here she is after much family debate, but she doesn't seem too disappointed.

She sees our journey to America as one of the most exciting things she has ever done, the trip of a lifetime. Her brother and sister were too established in the routines of life in Dorking. But once Priscilla heard her mother and father were going, there was absolutely no way she was staying behind.

She wanted to know all about my relationship with William—where we met, what I first thought of him, how I knew he was the one. She talked about a boy back home whom she had to say goodbye to in Dorking; she seems hopeful that he will maybe make the journey to America someday but also doesn't appear to be too upset if it doesn't work out for him.

We laughed about the food, how thankful we are for it even though it's utterly dreadful. It helps her to pretend that the serving of beans is a delicious fresh salad with greens from the garden; the cold pork becomes a delicate cut of warm venison served with sauce. We laughed coming up with thoughts of what they would serve us for dessert. Definitely some kind of fresh fruit pudding, or, if we were lucky, a choice sugar cake topped with strawberries. It made the evening so much fun—I told her how my recipe book is full of scrumptious desserts, and once we get settled, she can come over for lessons in cooking. Won't that be fun!

You would like her so much, Jaqueline. She is bright and funny and full of ideas and energy and life and enthusiasm. She is friendly and confident. I am glad to make her acquaintance.

Saturday, September 16

But seek ye first the kingdom of God, and his righteousness; and all these things shall be added unto you.
— Matthew 6:33

Dear Jaqueline,

Things I am grateful for today: 1) warm woolen socks we chose not to pack in the trunk below; 2) the warmth of holding a fresh cup of tea in my hands; 3) all that I'm learning about motherhood from living in close quarters with this many women and children. It occurs to me that God has called this unique group of women together for a purpose. Each woman is unique in her own story—they are teaching me so much.

My dearest Mary Brewster—what an incredible friendship we have had over the years. She is like a sister to me in every sense of the word, laughing at my jokes while other women think me strange or distant. I never would survive this journey without her. What a blessing she is. But being a neighbor and traveling together with this friend are two totally different things. For example, we're both early risers, but once awake, she immediately jumps into action, grabs her cup of tea, and is off and running, talking, making the day happen. I, on the other hand, am desperate to find a few moments of quiet time after I wake up. Without those few moments to stabilize my thoughts, my entire day can be a shamble. I like to get my tea, read, and have my moments of stillness before the day carries me away. We are most incompatible in this sense but are learning to respect each other's boundaries. It's a side we have never seen of one another. Almost her entire day is spent seeing to the needs of the boys. They are quite well-behaved but still quite needy. Her servants, Richard and little Mary, have special needs of their own, and although they are trying to be independent, one can see that they respond well to even the slightest bit of mothering.

There's Alice Rigsdale, who acts like a grandmother to all the children. While she's now in her late sixties and never raised any children of her own, she has this winsome personality that attracts children of all ages. She has this uncanny ability to entertain the toddlers with stories and funny faces. And then her understanding heart also meets the needs of any teenager who can't relate to a parent. What a gift she is to our growing community.

Three of our women, including Aunt Susanna, are close to their birth event. I think they are a special breed of brave. With no midwife on board, we have all pledged our service and are watching them, guarding them, protecting them. Each woman has selected four or five women who will serve as their main helpers. Some of us understand their needs more than others do. Thankfully they have all been through childbirth at least once, and that experience will help, but we are praying for easy, painless birth events for each of them. There will not be much downtime for any of them no matter what their experience.

I've mentioned Mary Allerton. She may arguably be the toughest one of us all. It was just last February when she and Isaac buried their infant. I think the grief she experienced during that loss was probably greater than any of us knew at the time. To know the joy of holding a newborn, then helplessly watching their ability to stay alive simply drift away. . . I can tell it was devastating, the type of experience that alters your perspective on life. She is a woman of great faith and dearly loves her role as mother. I am pleased for her and Isaac that God has blessed them with another baby so soon after that loss.

Mary was hopeful that her sister-in-law, Sarah, would come with her two daughters, but Sarah preferred to wait and come once our village is established. Her husband, Degory Priest, is traveling with us, but Sarah felt that the security of an established settlement was critical to raising her family. In spite of missing Sarah's company, Mary talks about her new friendships since the journey began and how she is gaining strength from the women of the *Mayflower.* Isn't it interesting how God pushes each of us out of our comfort zones and meets our needs in unexpected ways?

I've also formed a quick friendship with Sarah Eaton and sometimes give her a break from taking care of her one-year-old, Samuel. He reminds me so much of little John, with his blond curls and smile. Little John will have a wonderful playmate when he arrives next year.

I admire Sarah's courage in bringing him along. But she had no alternative, no family to leave him with. She sometimes seems a bit distant, as if she's hesitant to open up or not yet comfortable enough to share much of her past or what she's feeling. She's not really an outsider, having joined the journey from Leiden, but she came from Bristol and was not long enough with us in Leiden to fully integrate into our group. She and her husband, Francis, only lived in Leiden for about a year, so her life has changed dramatically, first with a marriage and a move to Leiden and then with a baby and now with another move. She seems bright and is always cheerful, but I imagine it's challenging to be dealing with that much chaos in one's life in such a short period of time.

Just now I am watching Sarah do all her morning chores while carrying Samuel. He is held close to her chest with this strap-like thing that wraps snugly around his back and then ties around her back. It's amazing. He has been fed and is nestled comfortably in the straps and is now starting to nod off. He loves to chew on the strap. He looks up at her, and she briefly speaks to him. He looks over at me, and I wave to get his smile. He looks back up at her, and his eyes start to droop. He is getting tired. Her hands are completely free because of this strap contraption. I also notice she has a satchel on her shoulder that is just the right size to hold almost anything she will need at any moment of the day. The wonder is that while she is carrying him, she gently jostles him back and forth, rocks him to sleep with her easy movements, all the while doing her chores, cleaning dishes, sorting clothes. What an amazing woman. Her ability to do three things at once is what captures my attention. I will need to point this out to William as something I would like him to make for me as our family grows.

It has been interesting to watch how God has bonded the women from Leiden and the women from England, even in our first month together. The women from our congregation were bound by our common desire for leaving. We saw the influences of Dutch customs and language having a negative impact on the children. It seems many of the women from England joined this journey for the same reason. While they may not completely agree with our beliefs, they have felt God's calling to a new way of living. Their commitment to structure their lives and the lives of their children according to the scriptures is the driving force that becomes our common bond. We may be a mixed group of personalities, but our bond is to raise our families in a community based on Christian principles—not the Christian principles that the Church of England was pushing, but the principles we read in the Bible. We have found a common bond and, indeed, friendship in serving meals side by side and caring for children. God is using this time on the ship together to form deep friendships that I know will carry over into our new community. While the initial plans for the new community included a section of town for the Leideners and a separate section for those from England, I can tell even now that the plan may be revised.

Thursday, September 21

Greater is he that is in you, than he that is in the world.
— 1 John 4:4

Jaqueline,

Today we are stunned, saddened, and thankful. Is it possible to feel all of those emotions at the same time? How is that even possible? We have witnessed God's amazing and incredible power but in a most tragic and unexpected way.

As I mentioned, since we entered deep water, several of us have struggled with sickness. One of the sailors, I don't even know his name, has been unfriendly to many of the passengers. But let me be clear, I don't mean just unfriendly. He bullied. He heckled. He humiliated our passengers, picking on poor souls who already felt miserable. He terrorized the decks with curses in a mean and most inappropriate way. His ranting and raving and carrying-on went to the point of obsession. And why did he behave like this? I have no clue.[16]

He was a bearded, repulsive man who reminded William of one of the town drunks in Leiden. He might not have even known what he was saying or doing. I've never seen a demon-possessed man, but he might have been. I pitied him. Why did he have to carry on so and frighten adults and children alike? There was nothing gained by his torments. I never ran into him on the upper deck, but we'd hear him swearing and complaining loudly to anyone who would listen about the weak passengers below and how he looked forward to tossing each one of their carcasses overboard before the journey's end.

At first, his utterances were annoying. Some of our men were bold enough to approach him the other day and kindly asked him to stop his profanity and insolent behavior. It only encouraged him more. He laughed and carried on with his threats, making all uncomfortable. He must have been an unhappy man indeed. A poor soul he was, trapped in his own pitiful attempt to feel better than those of us not used to the waves of deep water. Did he have something against us? We'd done nothing to harm him. We prayed daily for strength to withstand the man's torments and prayed for God to calm his hateful spirit.

I'll spare you the graphic details, but the man's actual curses against our seasickness rose up and fell back down on his own head over the last few days. We are not quite certain of what afflicted him, but we heard him all through the night. He sounded in a horrible desperate way. Dr. Fuller offered his assistance at one point in the evening. When he returned to our group a couple hours later, he had a look of horror and was unable to explain what he had seen. He said only that God appeared to be stripping the man of his power to harm anyone. Perhaps what appeared to be an instrument of Satan rearing his ugly head proved to be the grounds God was looking for to demonstrate his authority over our small but mighty group.

This morning we awoke to a deathly silence. We prepared the morning meal and moved about, wide-eyed, without a word, almost afraid to inquire. Even the waves were strangely quiet. Elder Brewster mentioned God's warning in Zephaniah 1:7. "Hold thy peace at the presence of the Lord God: for the day of the Lord is at hand."

Finally, Master Jones himself came down to speak to us and brought three of his crew. They spoke of the man passing on during the night and were apologetic for the sailor's behavior. The news has shaken our entire group of passengers and all the crew as well. All suspect this man's sudden affliction and ultimate death are a result of the just hand of God acting on our behalf. Many interpret this as a warning against anyone who persecutes us. The crew has vowed to work together to restore peace to the ship again.

Elder Brewster offered assistance in seeing the man's body committed to the deep. William later told me that watching that man's body disappear under the ocean waves was strangely eerie. I'm not sure William will ever be able to erase that image from his mind. Down the body went and then was completely gone. Did he fall deep into eternal darkness? Did the man hopefully repent in his last moments? Did he experience separation or a reunion in heaven? Was he accompanied by the dark hooded presence of death or the angel of light and life? I know God doesn't want any to perish, and I believe even those who call out his gracious name in the last few moments of life are saved. They may miss the blessing of his faithful presence while living but at least are saved from the eternal pit.

No one knew the man well enough to even speak aloud about his life, but Elder Brewster offered a few fitting words for death and last rites. I am thankful his words focused on the saving power of Jesus. We can only pray the man experienced forgiveness of sin and now knows fully the resurrection power of the risen Lord. The man received a traditional firing of the gun. I'm not so sure that Master Jones would have bothered with that, if not for Elder Brewster's insistence.

It has been a humbling experience for all of us, passengers and crew alike. Almost everywhere we go, the wicked flourish, and we wonder why. But here God chose to quench the situation. In an odd sort of way, his discipline of this man could serve to encourage us. But at the same time I find myself wrestling with these characteristics of my God. And I'm not meaning to be disrespectful in any way. But to see God's mercy toward some and God's judgment so clearly aimed at another seems a startling contradiction. How does one make sense of God's wrath against sin and God's love for sinners in the same moment? We do know God to be perfect in all his characteristics, trustworthy in his judgment as well as in his love. He's not really all one or all the other. He's both merciful and holy. I find that I have to accept all of his characteristics, not just the ones that make sense to me.

And then I wonder whether our prayers for justice, our prayers for relief from suffering of the man's tongue, had anything to do with God's justice. Did God choose to intervene in this way because of our prayers? Do we feel triumph because of this? We are not a vengeful people. We felt no hatred toward this man. We asked the man to stop what he was doing. Did the man have a history of criticizing those who believe as we do? Did something happen in his past to make him act so hateful toward us? I hate to think that my prayers could have brought a dreadful consequence on a man, but God acts on our behalf. We prayed according to his direction, and I believe God directly acted in response to our prayers. It's mysterious and humbling. Such a swift judgment. I pray the man had an opportunity to repent. I pray he made his peace with God in his last moments. One thing we are certain of is that God hears and responds to the prayers of his suffering people.

When we are afraid, we can look back and mark this as a point when we have been convinced beyond a shadow of doubt that the Lord goes before us whether the way is smooth or rough. When we suffer, we can be reminded that God has a bigger picture in mind. We can lift up our requests and concerns to God; he will provide, and we will trust him for the outcome. This could have ended differently; we were expecting his curses to increase and intensify, but God chose to show us that evil forces will not stand up against his plan.

In this we have witnessed God's faithfulness firsthand. While humbled, we are strengthened and confident that he will show us this facet of his character over and over and over again before this journey's end. I pray this news is not disturbing to you, Jaqueline, but instead brings you great comfort. The God of all creation is watching over us and will see our group safely to the destination. We are safe in his mighty hands.

Saturday, September 23

For I know the thoughts that I think toward you, saith the Lord, thoughts of peace, and not of evil, to give you an expected end.

Then shall ye call upon me, and ye shall go and pray unto me, and I will hearken unto you.

And ye shall seek me, and find me, when ye shall search for me with all your heart.

And I will be found of you, saith the Lord: and I will turn away your captivity, and I will gather you from all the nations, and from all the places whither I have driven you, saith the Lord; and I will bring you again into the place whence I caused you to be carried away captive.

— Jeremiah 29:11–14

Dear Jaqueline,

The sea is quiet. I'll stay in bed as long as possible, because I cherish these quiet moments. The only sound is the lapping of the waves against the hull. I can close my eyes and visualize the ship, sails wide, moving closer to our land. It won't be long before a young one cries out. Soon after that, children will start running up and down the middle aisle, and the morning activities will all fall in place. My stomach aches, and I want to stretch my legs, but I dare not lose this precious moment of quiet and peace.

My thoughts go out to you and to little John, and I am thankful again for God's leading us to leave him with you. I can't even imagine if I were caring for him in the midst of the hardship we have already experienced. Only God in all his wisdom would have known the best place for little John was with you. I know we are missing out on many of his developments this year. Remember your promise to keep track of every sentence he starts to speak and every funny thing you would know I want to know. Speak to him daily of the Lord's love and protection of him, our love for him, and how much we are looking forward to being together again.

I spend a lot of time thinking about all the children on this ship and each of their personalities. What a strong community of children we will have in the new land. Sometimes I try to imagine this trip from their perspective. There are close to thirty children, each one with his or her own unique story. Some of the older children like to lead the games, playing Cobb's castle, ninepins, and quoits. Others love to help the younger ones with preparing meals, reading, and knitting.

Without even being asked, they all help wherever they can—with meal preparation and cleanup, with dishes, with getting needed water and supplies. Many are quite remarkable in their level of maturity and responsibility. It's as if this journey gives them a newly discovered purpose. Some are not quite as mature and see only the excitement of this adventure. Some are so young they will have little to no recollection of the life we left behind and little, if any, memory of this time on the ship. Some have had to be reprimanded for behavior, and that always seems to have an effect on the whole group.

For the most part they are all healthy, except for Butten. He, maybe the sweetest among them, is not in good condition at all. He seems determined to stay positive and to be an encouragement to the little ones. He is out here without his father or mother and yet is so full of courage and charm. He has made fast friends with the young Samuel Fuller, who will often help Butten from his bed to the meal table or will sometimes take him a meal if he's not feeling up to joining the group. When it's time for worship, there are men who assist and carry Butten to the ladder and another group of men on the ladder that lifts him up to yet another group of men waiting on deck to carry him to our gathering. Dr. Fuller doesn't quite know what ails Butten but says it is not contagious, so we are hopeful he will recover quickly once we get to shore.

Butten is one of several who have never known true love of a parent. My heart especially goes out to those children. They know too much already about rejection, abandonment, and survival on their own. To think that they've never known a father who tells them stories or wrestles them to the ground or the security of running to a mother when something upsets them. It is sad that they have absolutely no idea what it means to grow up and flourish in a safe and loving home, no idea that God, who knows the number of hairs on their heads, considers their lives more treasured than the sparrows'.

The four More children are fascinating. Richard and little Mary. . . you should see them together. They are always looking out for one another and even sleep side by side. Jasper is flourishing in the care of the Carvers, as is Ellen in the care of the Winslows. Even though they are separated in their family assignments, they have a unique bond, a tie of love and protection that runs deep between the four unlike any I've seen elsewhere. These four, more than any others, were pleased when we consolidated our two groups into one ship. At worship they stand together and always seem to be looking for a way to support one another.

It's a relief that both the Brewster boys treat Richard as if he were their own brother. It would be a cruel circumstance for him if their attitude were different, but they've taken him in as one of their own. And little Mary... I'd like to scoop her up as my own. She is animated in her storytelling, and most days she talks nonstop. She is at that wonderful age of being able to carry on a conversation and loves any adult who takes time to listen to her. She often crawls into William's lap when Elder Brewster reads from the Bible. I am pleased for little Mary that in spite of her horrible situation, she has a loving brother to lean on and is finding a stable fatherly influence in Elder Brewster and William. I don't know how much of her family's tragic tale she is even fully aware of.

Theirs is a horrific story and is only whispered about here. Bits and pieces have been gathered from Carver, and William says that their father is not their biological father, that their mother and father were married as part of a family arrangement, totally against both of their wills, a marriage destined for trouble from the beginning. William speculates the mother was deeply in love with another man and that all four children are his. It's heartbreaking and bewildering to consider...four precious children, casualties of a family scheme, sent away by their father, to be distributed like packages amongst our *Mayflower* families. And their poor mother. Carver says the mother likely doesn't even know where her children are. The horror of waking up one morning to find that without your knowledge, someone had taken your four children. Who would even do that? I imagine she cries out for them every day.

The children speak little of it, but I know Richard and little Mary miss their mother in a terrible way. To think they have had to struggle with trying to make sense of such nonsensical circumstances at a young age. I can't even imagine the nightmares these children live with. And what memories do they have of their mother? Do they find comfort in hearing the truth of God's sovereignty and control of all circumstances? Although servants now, do they realize God may have rescued them for a greater purpose?

They face each day with amazing courage and strength; it is a blessing that they can look out for one another. Whatever has happened in their past is serving to bring them closer together. They may not ever see their mother again, but God their heavenly Father is keeping them safe, and they are learning a new way of life in a safe community.

Little Mary talks of writing to her mother to see if she will join them in America. I pray they have an opportunity to meet again. Again, we have only bits and pieces of the story, but sometimes we hear the children talking about this other man with great respect. It seems he took a great deal of interest in them and spent time playing with them and building a relationship with them. As they learn to live with the truth of what has happened, perhaps they will have an opportunity to get to know their true father better.

In the meantime, William and I seem to be in a unique position to encourage these young ones. In an unusual way they, in return, are a help to us in coping with missing little John so desperately. Once we get settled in our own home and are united with little John again, we will have time to think about having another child, and I believe a little girl would be a perfect addition to our family. I may even like to name her Mary.

Monday, September 25

And of Benjamin he said, The beloved of the Lord shall dwell in safety by him; and the Lord shall cover him all the day long, and he shall dwell between his shoulders.
— Deuteronomy 33:12

Dear Jaqueline,

There is no visible lightning or thunder yet, so we hope the approaching storm will be short. I am in my bunk now, but earlier, from my spot on the upper deck, I was able to watch us approach the storm front and could see there was no going around it. The front stretched far to the north and the south, dense and dark, blackness warning of a coming danger. Once we passed under the front, layer upon layer of clouds draped in various shades of gray floated quickly past us as if in a hurry to move out of the way. Then the sky turned into one solid sheet of gray, and rain poured down in buckets.

Master Jones has since sent out word that we are strictly forbidden on the upper deck, but there is no place to hide from the rain out here in open water. Rain is pounding on the upper deck, and I watch it pour through the ladder opening and make its way to the lower decks. Waves are rough and unnerving, unlike any we have experienced on the journey yet. They are massive and toss our ship back and forth. Winds are howling, so there will be little sleep if this continues through the night. I love you, dear Jaqueline, and know you are praying for us. I cling tightly to William's hand and also to the very hand of God, holding on to his abounding grace and mercy.

Tuesday, September 26

And, behold, there arose a great tempest in the sea, insomuch that the ship was covered with the waves: but he was asleep.

And his disciples came to him, and awoke him, saying, Lord, save us: we perish.

And he saith unto them, Why are ye fearful, O ye of little faith? Then he arose, and rebuked the winds and the sea; and there was a great calm.

But the men marvelled, saying, What manner of man is this, that even the winds and the sea obey him!

— Matthew 8:24–27

Dear Jaqueline,

Reporting the aftermath of yesterday's storm: there was nowhere to hide from the drenching rain. William and I huddled in one bunk under our thickest wool blanket, but there was absolutely no way to stay dry. Families up and down the walkway squeezed in close together. We covered children, animals, food, furniture, anything that could possibly get under cover with sheets, blankets, towels, anything that could possibly provide shelter. But we were not well prepared for that amount of rain. I thought the upper deck would shield us somewhat, but water poured in from every possible opening and began rising all around us.

We were helpless to protect our belongings. Many are now complaining of things that are ruined. I feel sorry for Elder Brewster—his favorite chair broke during the chaos of the storm, but he is hopeful it can be repaired. Many of our things will dry out and recover. We are all safe. No one was injured. What is most noticeable to me is the deck boards that have been scrubbed clean, both here on the between level and up above on the main level. Gone is the stench of early sickness. Gone is an entire layer of filth and debris. I have a new appreciation for the cleansing power of a downpour. It's as if they've been washed by heavenly hands.

We spent most of today recovering from the waterlogged chaos and wringing out every soaked article of clothing and attempting to dry out everything drenched from the storm. During our periods of rest, Stephen Hopkins found center stage and retold his tales of traveling. He is a funny older man with a salt-and-pepper beard. You'd never know he's in his early sixties, because he's fit as a fiddle, bounding with energy and strength. He has amazing tales and excellent storytelling skills that bring his stories to life. The deep worry lines across his brow are perhaps the only indication that his stories are true-to-life experiences. The children never seem to tire of hearing his stories, and today he provided welcome relief from the exhausting trial of that first storm.

Hopkins is our only passenger who has previously been to Virginia. His first trip there was on a ship similar in size to our *Mayflower*. It carried 140 people or so, including ten women and their children. They traveled with a group of seven ships that took supplies and a fresh group of strong men to assist with rebuilding the struggling Virginia Colony. The ships traveled together for more than a month, but then they encountered a horrific storm, and four of the ships were separated from the mass. He describes howling winds, drenching rain, and waves so huge they threatened to tear his ship apart. He tells of screaming and crying, organized teams working together to bail and haul water, sleeping in one-hour shifts, for days on end, desperately trying to stay ahead of the torrential rain that filled their ship day after day, night after night. No access to food in the deck below. Sailors doing their best to keep the ship afloat, running, yelling. Passengers doing their best to keep the panic at bay but hungry, thirsty, cold, and wet. He says the storm continued on for three or four days. I can't even imagine that.

Of course, the older children are thrilled with his tales. Many of them long for adventures like his, adventures they can call their own. Little Mary, looking for a safe place, climbs in my lap when Hopkins starts his tales. When she needs to, she can bury her tiny face in my arms. I listen to his stories and am chilled to the core. But I tell myself it is a good reminder that even though we were completely drenched and overwhelmed by that first storm yesterday, it was nothing compared to what the sea is capable of. It's a strange sensation, hearing Hopkins telling his true-to-life actual survival story while we huddle in the lower deck of the ship, bobbing around in the middle of nowhere. It would be different if we were sitting around a cozy fire in the neighborhood park. It would not have quite the same effect on my emotions. Reality has an odd effect on heightening all senses.

He remembers with amazing details their shipwreck in the Bermuda islands, months of scrounging for food and shelter on the island, rebuilding their ship, and eventually arriving in Virginia. He was able to work in Jamestown for several years and was one of the key contributors to the rebuilding of that colony. He is extremely honored to have an opportunity to return to America and start a new colony. He adds a wealth of experience and knowledge to our measly group of inexperienced travelers.

Thankfully our path is not taking us anywhere near the Bermudas. But if Hopkins has not exaggerated, I wonder whether we will be able to endure such a storm in our path. I trust that God is mapping out each inch of our sail across this huge expanse of water, so I will place my trust in him and him alone.

William learned that Hopkins left his two children and first wife behind in London on that first trip to America. Apparently, his wife did well for several years in his absence, caring for the children, running a shop, and living on those wages, but then she died unexpectedly, which is why Hopkins returned home from Jamestown. He gathered the children, moved to London, met Elizabeth, and quickly remarried. I don't know his new wife well, but she is quickly gaining my respect as another amazing woman. She calmly listens while he is in the height of his boisterous tales. She laughs lightheartedly as if maybe she knows the stories are a bit exaggerated for entertainment. She manages three children with noticeable ease, and two of them are not even her own. The Hopkinses now have a two-year-old of their own named Damaris. Isn't that a beautiful name? There are so many names to pick for a girl. I would have to pick Mary, of course, even though there are already many Marys in our group: Mary Brewster, Mary Allerton, Mary Mullins, Mary Chilton. It doesn't matter. My girl will have to be named Mary. Anyway, Damaris is as gentle and calm as her name implies, very much like her mother. And very much a contrast to her father.

As I said, Hopkins is notably a good storyteller and obviously devoted to his children, but he is also known to be rowdy and loud at times. He is even rumored to drink heavily in the evenings. Can you picture that? The man I described is the same man who read psalms and chapters at Sunday services for the Virginia Company. Yes, that was his official job on his first trip to America—the minister's clerk! God has a sense of humor sometimes. Then take that picture of him and contrast it with a father playing with three well-behaved and slightly frail children. All of his children seem to soak in every word he says—they take our troubles at sea all in stride. Maybe being with their father is the only thing that really matters, especially to the older two who were left behind on his first trip.

William says Hopkins paid a high price to bring Elizabeth and the three children on this voyage, but under no circumstances would he leave them behind, even with Elizabeth being six and a half months along in her pregnancy. I've heard Hopkins helped birth both a girl and a boy on that first trip to Virginia, and he plans to help Elizabeth when she's ready. I must try to get to know her better in the coming months, as she will need extra hands when the new one arrives.

Sunday, October 1

He sent from above, he took me, he drew me out of many waters.
— Psalm 18:16

Dear Jaqueline,

We nearly lost our first passenger today. It all happened so suddenly that we didn't know exactly what we were dealing with until it was all over.

We had fierce rain again from the first light of day, so Elder Brewster had to cancel our morning service. Large waves crashed over the main deck. I found at times that the wind and rain, waves and rocking, lulled me into a stupor. At other times I heard "the monster" roar outside and knew we were totally helpless, at the mercy of our God who controls both wind and waves.

Many in our area were sick from the waves, and the smell was dreadful. Add to that smell crying and wailing and carrying-on, and on top of that the continual pounding of the rain and wind and thunder and lightning. It's not so bad when a storm lasts only a couple hours, but a full day of it can push one to the limits. The smells and sounds were starting to bother me, and I found myself longing for fresh air even if it meant getting drenched in the process. I am certain this is why John Howland went up on deck, so I fully understand.

The first miracle was that some of the crew were close by and saw what happened. Within a couple minutes of entering the main deck, Howland slipped and went down, falling hard on the deck boards just as a large wave crashed over the side and swept the deck clean. The crew tried to reach him before he was swept off and out into the deep.

It's a second miracle that Howland somehow caught hold of one of the ropes hanging from the deck of the ship and was able to hang on with all his strength. Of course, we all heard the commotion and the crew shouting orders, but we didn't know what had happened. Carver was the first to realize the shouting was all about Howland, so several of our men raced up. Howland had drifted far from the ship and went far under the waves several times, but still he somehow managed to hang on to that rope. Our men worked with the crew to slowly pull him in and were able to get him close to the side of the ship. While waves crashed overhead, they lowered the boat hook and dragged Howland back to safety.

Thankfully the wind and rain have subsided for now, but it does not look good for Howland. He is downstairs now, breathing and lying quietly. He is as white as a ghost, maybe from the shock of the experience or the chill of the water or both. He is so loved, and Dr. Fuller is concerned that he will not survive the night. He is a strong young man, and we are in prayer for his full recovery. We know and trust the healing power of God, but it will require a third miracle to continue this dramatic saving and provide the strength Howland needs to survive.

William agrees it was the smell that finally drove Howland upstairs for fresh air in that spontaneous moment. At first I supported that thought—maybe he had his fill of the high-pitched whining of the storm, but now a part of me wonders whether Howland was testing God. He has so much going for him—good looks, smarts, many good friends—and yet he's lost so much. He has no family. He is here with the Carvers and has made close friends with their servants Dorothy and Desire. But like any young man, he might question what in the world God is doing. If indeed he were testing God, he certainly got an answer today. Regardless, it was not a good decision, and we have all learned from his experience. Desire and Dorothy haven't left his side. Dr. Fuller is attending to him, so he is in good hands, but this has unnerved us all.

Monday, October 2

*And, behold, I am with thee, and will keep thee in all places whither thou
goest, and will bring thee again into this land; for I will not leave thee, until I
have done that which I have spoken to thee of.*
— Genesis 28:15

My dear Jaqueline,

Howland is starting to show signs of recovery, so that is a relief, but now
my stomach is not behaving. While I am not one to complain, I may simply
stay in my bunk all day. My legs ache from lack of activity. I am weak and
weepy and tired of being cramped up in this tiny space and darkness.

The seas are rough, and everything seems overwhelming today. My
thoughts have wandered to all the wonderful things we've left behind. I didn't
realize how much I would miss my home. William tells me I shouldn't even
think of these things at this point in the journey. In his mind it's better to not let
one's mind wander far from the present, so I will share my thoughts with you.

My list of things I miss:
- Long walks around the neighborhood in the early evening
- Our small summer garden full of onions and lettuce
- Fresh blackberries growing in the stretch of grasses behind our
  house
- The nearby canal with ducks and geese and sometimes a small
  heron that fed on the frogs
- Our trips to the open market, where artists and strolling musicians
  played for a coin
- Our sweet conversation and laughs over the silliest of things

I wish for a moment I could catch a glimpse of Momma's amazingly
beautiful blue eyes. In an odd way I am comforted by these thoughts. They
make this horrible day more tolerable. The images are so close I feel as if I
could reach out and touch them all. But nothing can change where I am right
now, and you are far, far away. It is lonely here without you. Yes, I have
William and my neighbors and new friends, but I am feeling a bit lost at sea,
with nothing much to ground me.

I better not even start listing the things I miss about little John. That
would lead to misery, and I might not recover. I do so miss you and all the
precious pieces of the life we had together. Lord help me through this day.

Sunday, October 8

He that dwelleth in the secret place of the most High shall abide under the shadow of the Almighty.

I will say of the Lord, He is my refuge and my fortress: my God; in him will I trust.

Surely he shall deliver thee from the snare of the fowler, and from the noisome pestilence.

He shall cover thee with his feathers, and under his wings shalt thou trust: his truth shall be thy shield and buckler.
— Psalm 91:1–4

Dear Jaqueline,

Elder Brewster canceled morning services. Perhaps we will regroup this afternoon, but we are exhausted, physically and mentally, being on the back side of a frightening storm, and I thank you again for your prayers. I have felt your prayers and God's peace, but we are not the same group of people we were a few days ago, before the storm. That much I know for certain. I have had little time over the last couple days to even think about home or feeling sick or anything, so that has been good, but every experience, every day threatens to drive us further and further into despair.

I am not even sure how I would describe the storm we have lived through. . . horror, chaos, and hell may be the best descriptors. Apparently at certain times of the year it's not unusual to encounter ferocious winds out here. Master Jones explains it as warm air currents from the south meeting cold air currents from the north. The crew isn't surprised to find a treacherous storm out here in the middle of the ocean. I am still in shock, however, that we ran smack into a massive storm.

For two or three days we noticed waves growing both in size and intensity. Our progress slowed. Master Jones consulted with the men. Of course, he had no way to measure the magnitude of the storm, but he was convinced that to steer north would add too much time to our journey. Since we were already delayed, all determined we would stay the course. But the waves increased; at times our speed slowed to almost nothing. And then the rain and wind started. Two full days of it. No progress. No sun. No stars. Screaming winds and water pouring in from all directions, saltwater sloshing in and welling up all around our feet. All we could do was hold tightly to one another in the dark. Daylight hours brought little relief.

At one point the winds shifted and drove straight from the west. The sky, which had been mostly gray from the low-hanging clouds, took on a dark, sinister look. Master Jones ordered the deck to be cleared. Exhausted, the crew secured the masts and sheets, and all took shelter in our area. And yes, you are correct, that meant no one was guiding the ship. We were completely at the mercy of the wind and waves. It struck a chord of horror in many of us.

Families huddled. Husbands and wives wept openly. Elder Brewster and William went into discussions with Master Jones, so I gathered with Mary Brewster and other women and children and began prayers. My dearest Mary—she has more courage than anyone I know. It is amazing how her fearless nature spread a peace and calmness over that little group. We could hear the men yelling over the sounds of the storm, discussing the terror and destruction and dangers we were facing, but Mary helped us focus on the Word of God. Her words of encouragement in the midst of that turmoil renewed my sense of hope. "God will see us through this storm," she said, "as he has with every storm we've encountered so far." The woman truly has no fear, I tell you. If God were going to take her right here and now, what would she have to fear? She would be home with her Savior and singing in heaven, so if that's the worst that would happen, so be it. I was never so grateful for her encouraging spirit. She reminded us of the violent storms endured by the apostle Paul and how he wrote of being "exceedingly tossed with a tempest" (Acts 27:18). If God could see Paul through such a storm, then God would see us through as well.

Sometimes our ship rocked from front to back, sometimes it rolled from side to side, and sometimes it seemed to twist. I was certain we were doomed and expected the ship to break in half. All I could do was pray for mercy. We literally feared for our lives and wondered whether this were the end we were all fated to.

What kept going through my mind, though, was, "Why would Jesus lead us this far, to this end? A death out in the middle of the ocean? Halfway to our destination? To what purpose would that serve? To what glory?" I sensed God's mighty hand was at work, not only in the details of our journey but in leading us further, deeper into trust. The women sang every psalm we could think of. We pulled the children in close. What lessons were they learning about their God and his ability to rise above the circumstances presented to them?

I know we made it through one full day like that and thought we were doing pretty well considering, but then the roar of the monster increased in intensity. Lightning strikes on the ocean became more severe than any I have ever experienced; they struck in front of us, behind us, all around us. You know how thunder sometimes sounds delayed after lightning strikes? Let's just say there is no delay when it strikes on open water.

And then amid fierce waves and constant clapping of thunder came this terrifying, loud crack of splitting wood—I will never forget that sound. I thought for sure the ship would go down. Had we been struck by lightning? John Hooke was seated in the middle of the deck and was the first one to shout. "It's the beam!" Master Jones and crew rushed over, and in the faint light of their lanterns we clearly saw the main structural beam, visibly bent and fractured from top to bottom.[17]

An entirely new wave of fear took hold. All I could do was sit in horror, listen, and watch it all unravel before my very eyes. I was physically frozen. Men shouted. Women screamed. Children cried all around me. And I couldn't move or speak. It was a moment of grave danger. Questions ran through my mind—would we make it through the storm? And if we did, would we even now be able to complete the journey at all? Several of the crew rebelled loudly, insisting they were not willing to risk their lives aboard a ship with a cracked main beam. Master Jones said the safest thing would be to turn back. Turn back? I couldn't even react; I couldn't believe what I was hearing. Words between our men and the crew grew as vicious as the high-pitched winds. It truly brought out the worst in us.

Elder Brewster desperately tried to keep the group calm. Speaking loudly to be heard above the sounds of wind and waves, he tried reasoning with Master Jones and the crew. "Turning back is not an option. After so many days on the water? That would mean an end to our contract. How would we pay back those who loaned us the money? We would not find another ship to sail at this time of year. It would be spring before we could begin to make plans for another journey. Any delay at this point would make everything impossible."

And from out of nowhere Francis Eaton spoke up. He remembered the large iron screw brought along to be used for building our homes. He was thinking out loud but asked if anyone thought it was possible to try and leverage the screw against the weight of the sturdy beams. It could possibly hold the main beam in place to ride us through the storm. Master Jones quickly reacted, agreeing it was worth a try, and the men raced into action.

Mary startled me out of my stupor, and I helped her move all the children to the far end of the ship. Again we held hands, and many sang praises to our God, but I slipped into a daze again, and all I could do was sit and watch. It was a truly odd sensation. Six men carried the massive screw from storage into place by the beam. Several others helped carefully position the screw under the beam. Slowly, slowly they turned the screw's large wooden handle, and slowly, surely, they lifted that beam right back into place. I couldn't take my eyes off where that beautiful broken beam now stood straight and tall again, firmly in place. It was like watching God reach down from heaven and secure that broken beam with his own mighty hand. Stunning!

We were able to ride out the rest of the afternoon without further incident. Thunder and lightning eventually passed into the distance. After a time, Master Jones released the crew, and they raced upstairs and lifted the sails. Our ship caught wind, and we spent most of the afternoon in joyful tears and worship.

Looking back, I find it interesting to see how each one of us reacted differently to the situation. Elder Brewster praised God for providing insight to Eaton, guiding him to remember that iron screw. I silently praised God for changing the hearts of the crew—they simply forgot all those words and the discussion of turning around. What a good and mighty God we serve!

Early in the evening the strangest color filled the sky. It was a mixture of orange and yellow, a brilliant, glowing color. My dearest Mary, who doesn't even like to go on the main deck, followed me up the ladder without a word. We found the entire western sky ablaze. Somehow the setting sun in the west was hidden behind a thin layer of clouds, and we weren't sure whether the reflections were from the water or heaven itself. Before us, the clouds passed to the north and east, and they, too, were filled with the brilliant glow. It was one of those moments when God seemed present. Whatever he has planned for our future, he is worthy of our trust. We watched the sky for a long, long time and then returned to the group below.

I slept well last night, from exhaustion but also from grasping the fullness of the goodness of God's provision. A deep peace came from seeing his mighty hand at work, seeing his glory in the sky above and around me, watching as he transformed a crushing blow to the midship beam into a secure hold on a team with an ever-intensifying mission. It is an experience I will never forget. He saw us through that storm. He will see us through safely to land. I am confident of it.

The reality of the last couple days is that we are here in this small, small boat in the middle of the big, big ocean, and we have nowhere to hide but in the hand of our Savior. Only the mercy of God could see us through a storm like that. That storm showed me once again there's truly no place where I can't find his peace. There's truly no space where his love can't reach. It was a witness to our community and every nonbeliever aboard this ship that there's no end to his amazing grace. Even the crew joined us in worship today. I tell you the truth, Jaqueline, it was as if I could literally feel him holding me in his arms. Throughout that entire storm he never let go, never left my side, never stopped protecting me and loving me. He proves himself over and over. What an amazing God we serve.

Note: You and little John *must* travel earlier in the year when the danger of storms will be lower. You definitely would not have the stomach for that type of storm.

Tuesday, October 10

Trust in the Lord with all thine heart; and lean not unto thine own understanding.
In all thy ways acknowledge him, and he shall direct thy paths.
— Proverbs 3:5–6

Dear Jaqueline,

We are in trouble now. Two days of smooth sailing, and Master Jones called for consultation this morning. After studying all the instruments, he's thoroughly convinced that we are now off course, slightly north of our destination. I don't understand all the details, but he says it is due to the prevailing westerlies, strong winds that blow from west to east. Of course, such a wind could be a huge advantage to shipmasters sailing from America to England. Apparently catching a westerly can save days of travel, with speeds enhanced by the powerful winds. Unfortunately, sailing straight into a westerly is not ideal. Master Jones said his original plan was to steer north of the known westerly boundary as we headed west, and then he planned to capitalize on its benefits when the crew returned home to England. Apparently, the noted boundary has shifted.

You can imagine how disturbing this news is because we are contracted to work a very specific piece of land in Virginia. However, Master Jones strongly believes that if we continue due west to find land, we can then venture south along the coast to our planned destination in Virginia. So that is the plan of action now, and all agree—which is good because the days are taking their toll, and many do not have strength or fortitude for arguing.

Thursday, October 12

Charity suffereth long, and is kind: charity envieth not; charity vaunteth not itself, is not puffed up,
Doth not behave itself unseemly, seeketh not her own, is not easily pro-voked, thinketh no evil;
Rejoiceth not in iniquity, but rejoiceth in the truth;
Beareth all things, believeth all things, hopeth all things, endureth all things.
Charity never faileth.
— 1 Corinthians 13:4–8

Dear Jaqueline,

I don't know exactly where to begin, but I discovered that one of the ladies on board is a gossip. At this point I am literally feeling there is ab-solutely no one I can confide in, and I am more than ever missing your trust-worthy spirit. Don't get me wrong—I love these dear women. My neighbors and friends are becoming like sisters to me, but I'm learning the hard way that they are not all to be trusted like a sister.

It's almost embarrassing, but a couple days ago I was sitting with a few of the women, studying and sharing prayer requests. I thought it would be helpful to have prayer for my concerns about having a second child. My con-cerns are likely normal, but I've been anxious lately wondering how in the world I will manage two children when the time comes and how I will con-tinue to build my relationship with little John while developing a brand-new relationship with a second child. How will I find time for William while tak-ing care of two children? How will I find time for my Lord when every hour of my day will be stretched with family demands? How will I maintain rela-tionships with my friends and maintain a healthy balance? It has been over-whelming to think about, which is why I went ahead and shared it for prayer. I see these women with multiple children and simply don't know how I could do what they do.

Since there were only a few ladies present, I thought it might be safe to share my concern so they could lift it up in their private prayers for me. I always treat prayer requests as confidential, but apparently that's not a universal rule.

So, this afternoon I was helping with the older children's lessons, and Elizabeth Hopkins comes up to me and whispers, "I hear you're worried about having a second child. You don't need to be concerned. Take it from one who knows." She went on and on, not realizing I stopped listening after her first sentence. I wanted to ask, "Who did you hear that from?" But the words stuck in my throat. It must have been someone from that small group of women, and now I am feeling slightly betrayed. Am I taking this too seriously? If I had wanted the entire community to know and weigh in on my concern, I certainly could have asked. But now it appears I am the subject of gossip. It's slightly horrifying. If they want gossip, isn't there enough to talk about with the More children or the Billington family?

It's most difficult that there is little to no privacy in this group right now. So why would someone take a personal prayer request, one that was shared in confidence, and blurt it out for others to be made aware of? This has upset me, and I don't even know whom to be upset with. Maybe I'm too private of a person. Maybe the lesson is for me to learn that the only one I need to share my concerns with is God himself. If anything, I have learned a new respect for the words "just between you and me." If another woman shares something with me in confidence, I intend to hold it in absolute trust and respect that privacy.

Oh Lord, help me. I need to forgive and get past this, but it's a struggle.

Saturday, October 14

Jesus answered and said unto her, Whosoever drinketh of this water shall thirst again:
But whosoever drinketh of the water that I shall give him shall never thirst; but the water that I shall give him shall be in him a well of water springing up into everlasting life.
— John 4:13–14

Dear Jaqueline,

I know it's true on any given day that there is little I can do about things that happen in my life. Here on this ship, it is truer than ever—I have no real control over the way things go. All I can do is pray. So I pray for you at home, pray that Momma will somehow be at peace with my traveling so far away, pray for little John to grow and flourish in your care, pray for your strength and health to keep everything going without my help, pray for this journey, pray that our supplies will last, pray for these children to be encouraged, pray for wisdom for this crew, pray for patience and endurance and health for all passengers, pray for William to manage all the responsibility of being one of the congregation leaders, and pray for what lies ahead—our safe arrival, wisdom in getting settled, strength, and direction to quickly build our home before winter.

But would it amaze you to know that in spite of my limited prayers, he who holds the universe in his hands is so intimately aware of the needs of this little community? While we are specks of dust in comparison to his entire Kingdom, he is taking care of us, protecting us, leading us as if we're the only ones who matter.

I was having a dream right before I awakened this morning, so this image is fresh in my mind. I was standing on a shoreline with this vast body of water in front of me. I was not sure whether it was a river or a lake or a pond, but it was large enough that I couldn't see the other side. The sun was brilliantly bright, shimmering on the water, shining in my eyes, and I remember thinking that I was so anxiously awaiting someone's arrival. It was a peaceful and beautiful dream, and it has stayed in my mind all day. Because of what happened yesterday, it makes me think about how important it is to pray for even those I am not aware of, those whom God is making himself known to. While I am normally busy praying for my family and friends, he is busy drawing others to know him.

For example, yesterday one of the crew stopped William on the upper deck.[18] The man wanted to know more about this Christ we sing of and pray to. William said the man was like a thirsty sponge, soaking up everything William was able to share from the Word and his personal story. Elder Brewster joined the discussion, and before long word circulated below that they were speaking to a sailor on deck about Jesus. The man was raised with an understanding of God but in hearing our worship and prayers became convicted of his need for a Savior. He is a bit fearful that his crewmates will make light of his most serious decision, but I doubt it, especially in light of the sailor who died last month. This one seems well respected for his hard work and is some type of relative to Master Jones. Perhaps he will be able to shine a new light into a once dark space and bring others to know Jesus before this ship returns to England.

While we celebrate this young man's enthusiasm for God's Word, I see it as another example of what happens when God calls to a heart—there is no response other than to pick up and follow. Jesus called those first disciples by name. They left family and homes and never looked back. God called out to Paul, and his life was never the same. I don't know much about the story of this young man on our boat, but I do know that our God brought him to this moment and to this place to hear the good Word and see the Word at work in our lives. I truly believe God engineered this young man's circumstances to come to this exact, specific moment in time, when the man's heart and his needs and God's powerful redemption story came together.

Elder Brewster promised to formally baptize the young man when we get to shore, but he was anxious to be baptized right then. A few of us gathered, William pulled up a bucket of water from the ocean, and Elder Brewster baptized him on the upper deck in front of God and crew and community. It was a blessed sight to see the man's radiant smile, to see him cleansed of his past and shame and sin, now forgiven and ready to begin his new life with Jesus. I wonder how many of his friends will now follow in his footsteps and what will happen from this one man stepping forward in faith.

It gives me new motivation to pray now for all on this ship—for those who don't know Jesus to open their hearts to his direction and drawing power. I will pray his light will shine through us in our daily activities, in our worship, and in our courage, and I will pray that we can be the spark that he wants us to be right here on this ship. Our intent was to build a community on the coast that would speak of his love and light, but even in our going we carry this torch of his Spirit, which exudes the fragrance of his love and joy wherever we go. What an amazing God we serve!

Tuesday, October 17

Verily I say unto you, Whosoever shall not receive the kingdom of God as a little child, he shall not enter therein.
And he took [the little children] up in his arms, put his hands upon them, and blessed them.
— Mark 10:15–16

Dear Jaqueline,

What a celebration today! The Hopkins baby arrived, and we are much relieved. Although a bit fragile, the boy appears to be eating and resting well—his name is Oceanus, born with a huge wave of dark brown hair. His arrival brings excitement and renewal and perhaps the first hopeful moment we have had in many days.

We are all a bit giddy from lack of sleep, but both baby and Elizabeth are resting, so all seems right in the world. The ship sails are full. Even the clouds roll by in an easy, carefree manner. Last night William mentioned how calm the seas were, and together we watched the tiniest sliver of the moon peek out just before sunset.

Elizabeth's labor started shortly after. With this being her second delivery, she immediately recognized the signs of the sudden drop and water break. She quickly notified Mary Brewster, and within a matter of minutes our team had her ready and comfortable. Sarah Eaton stepped in and took Elizabeth's children down to her area. Dr. Fuller attended to Elizabeth, and Desire Minter stepped in to assist with the midwife skills she learned from her mother. We are a good team when we have a purpose.

Elizabeth's contractions were intense to start, but when darkness fell, her labor slowed. She had told us this second child might come quickly, but that was not God's plan. At one point, Dr. Fuller even said it might be a false labor, so we did not anticipate a long night, but there was no sleeping for anyone.

True to his word, Hopkins was by her side, tenderly holding Elizabeth's hand the entire time. His experience in traveling these waters before allowed him to be a calm encourager in those midnight hours. Never once did he raise his voice or even start to seem nervous or embarrassed or impatient. It was a side of him that we haven't seen before—quite loving and pleasant. He wasn't even the slightest bit concerned about expressing his deep love for her in front of a hundred passengers. I kept thinking what a brave soul Elizabeth was. She put all modesty aside and was fully aware that while she was lying there, an entire group of men and children and strangers sat a few feet away, all in frozen anticipation of what was happening, all experiencing this delivery right along with her, firsthand. That's not the delivery I would have wanted, but she was amazing. Her ability to stay focused on the task at hand was remarkable.

When the sky turned to morning blue, it was like a spring robin's-egg blue. Elizabeth's contractions returned in intensity. She expressed concern that she was not at full term but sensed the baby was determined. Nervously we listened to her cries of labor. Breathlessly we waited for the baby to arrive, praying for a safe delivery amid unusual circumstances. Time passed slowly. We tried to be encouraging, but anxiety was high. No one dared express aloud the question that was going through our minds—what would we do if something went wrong with the delivery?

In the end, the arrival happened quickly, and I will never forget that moment. The newborn cried out, and Dr. Fuller lifted him high for all to see. The entire ship broke out in cheers. Relief was visible.

I was overcome with emotion, nearly choked on my own tears, and had to step away from Elizabeth for a minute. When I saw that baby boy, all I could think about was little John. The images rushed in, and I was overcome with emotion—his face, his smile, images from his birth, you and Momma beside me. And then I remembered his first cry and holding him, tiny and wrapped, in that soft blue blanket. I was so relieved for Elizabeth but completely overwhelmed with missing little John at the same time.

Thankfully, William was nearby and held me while I cried away all those emotions and thoughts. Sweet William, always there when I need him. He may not show his emotions often, but he certainly understood my feelings and knew the right words to calm me down.

I know that nothing will ever be able to erase these precious thoughts we hold on to of little John. But there continue to be moments of uncertainty when I question our decision to leave him, to leave all of you. There is nothing we can do to change the decision now, but I honestly play it over and over and over in my mind. God seems to use those moments to strengthen me. He is always right there with me in those moments. And after a while, comforted by his peace and strength, I gain composure and get back to the reality of where we are, of where little John is, of where you are. I know I am not able to change these circumstances, and I am faced with making the most of my time here, praying that God will protect all of you, knowing that God is faithful, knowing that his plan and his timing are perfect. I am confident that he will bring us together again. Thank God for his mercy. Thank God for the peaceful waters we are in right now. Thank God for his mighty hand upon this family. Thank God for William.

The merriment all around is contagious and uplifting. Just know that my heart, my thoughts, are all of you. Master Jones has been ringing the ship bells all morning in celebration. Festivity is everywhere—children singing, fathers whistling, families laughing, couples dancing; this has been a tremendous lift to our spirits. For a few precious hours we have been united in breathing the fresh air of new life. What a gift. And what a handsome boy Elizabeth now has—tiny with eyes as blue and deep as the sea, all fingers and toes in place. Elder Brewster spoke a solemn and gracious prayer, a blessing over the family and its newest member. It gives me chills to think about, and I can still hear the crew singing up above and shouting to one another with renewed energy. I am so thankful for God's mercy and this safe arrival of Oceanus.

Thursday, October 19

The Lord is merciful and gracious, slow to anger, and plenteous in mercy.
He will not always chide: neither will he keep his anger for ever.
He hath not dealt with us after our sins; nor rewarded us according to our iniquities.
For as the heaven is high above the earth, so great is his mercy toward them that fear him.
As far as the east is from the west, so far hath he removed our transgressions from us.
— Psalm 103:8–12

Jaqueline,

I am completely torn about what to do. Today I was sorting through our important documents and found, of all things, an error on the receipt from our final payment for the journey. I don't know how I missed it before. I know that I checked the amounts we paid, and they all matched. I was watching that so closely, knowing exactly what we were committed to pay and checking to make sure it was marked "paid." This receipt is marked "paid in full," but then it jumped out at me that they missed the calculation. It's a small error, a difference of five pounds, because they didn't add the amounts properly. You'd think we would have noticed this earlier, but I guess in all the chaos of our last few days of packing, we weren't thinking clearly or paying close attention to these details.

But there it is. We have underpaid by five pounds. Let me repeat, we are talking about five pounds. The way I'm wrestling with it, you'd think it was five hundred pounds. But part of me sees this as one of those tests of my honesty—will I do the right thing and settle the difference with our recordkeeper immediately? I assume that even though we are thousands of miles away from London, the funds could get to the right party in due time. It's completely proper that we should pay the expected amount and not get away with paying less than what we owe. Or do I look at this as God's grace, showing me now that this was his hand, his way of saving us five pounds? Maybe he intends me to now use this amount for some important need on the journey? He is in charge of every penny we earn, and he knows we need every extra penny we can get. Maybe it's to be used for something I wouldn't normally be able to purchase? Maybe I should now use that amount to trade for fabric to make a new gown for little Mary?

Sometimes this standard of honesty is challenging. It shouldn't even be a question. When I get the wrong amount of change at market, I am quick to let the clerk know. I never want the clerk to come up shorthanded at the end of the day and have a supervisor look accusingly at him as to why there is a cash shortage. But no one has come asking us for this. And if I never speak a word about this, probably no one would notice this at all. No one would know except me and you and God above.

I'm writing this down in hopes that laying it out before you and God will help clear it all in my mind. I must be tired and not able to process this like I normally would. Is this the silliest thing you've read? I'll have to discuss it with William. It's his money too. That means one other person will know about this. But if I'm to figure out what to do, then I must consult him and make it a joint decision. I'll let you know what we decide to do.

Saturday, October 21

Therefore if any man be in Christ, he is a new creature: old things are passed away; behold, all things are become new.
— 2 Corinthians 5:17

Dear Jaqueline,

Today, after the noon meal, Agnes Tilley brought Humility by to see little Mary and Ellen. Even though she has no children of her own, Agnes is gifted at captivating the attention of children. She brought out her slate, and it was as if she opened a rainbow. The oohs and aahs and squeals of delight were contagious.

I've always heard of Agnes's talent for drawing but have never seen her in action as I saw today. The children sat patiently watching Agnes draw a series of lines and circles. Then Agnes made them guess what critter she was drawing. First it was a mouse eating cheese, then a parade of elephants, a dog wagging his tail, and a cat with his back arched. Suddenly the children started calling out names of their favorite animals to see if she could draw it. Her style is quite funny; each animal she drew seemed to have a funny characteristic, its own personality, all to the children's delight.

Then Agnes passed her slate to the children. It was the perfect distraction to get their minds off our daily struggles. For over an hour they poured all energy and restlessness into their drawings, carefully handling the slate and chalk, politely taking turns with the utmost of manners and kindness. It was a sight to see.

It was little Mary who captured my full attention. When it was her turn, she insisted I sit next to her while she worked on her drawing. I wasn't sure what she would draw. As difficult as her family life has been, I must have been expecting to see something dismal or loaded with deep hidden meanings of her family struggles. I sat with her, not really watching the drawing develop but more or less being there as a source of comfort. When she finished and shared her drawing, I sat there, quite stunned, for a minute or two. Her drawing was a sweet, sweet scene.

Proudly, she pointed out the bright sun that was shining, one character that was me, and another one that was William. She pointed out which one was her, and she was holding hands with Ellen, Jasper, and Richard. She drew in the Brewster family, and every character was smiling. It was confirmation to me of

God's goodness, his ability to "restore to you the years that the locust hath eaten" (Joel 2:25), actual visual proof that he has the power to make all things work for good. Here was proof that he had taken one of the saddest of stories and created hope and a bright future in the heart of this sweet little angel.

We will indeed have to ask Agnes Tilley to share her slate and chalk again.

Sunday, October 22

Thy word is a lamp unto my feet, and a light unto my path.
— Psalm 119:105

Dear Jaqueline,

It's been three months to the day since we left family and friends on the shore of Delfshaven, and the journey seems never-ending. If I didn't have my senses about me, I might let my mind play tricks and imagine that this is one big prank, that there is no Virginia or America, that there is no land on the other side of the ocean, that all those stories we heard about people who settled in the wilderness were just that. Stories. Maybe we are so far off course that we completely missed America and have veered far to the north or to the south. How would I even know? We completely put our trust in Master Jones and his crew. But what if their instruments are faulty? It could be one great scam, and they are waiting until we get weak enough to be rid of us all. What were we thinking? Our bodies get weaker by the day, which means our minds are losing sharpness and clarity.

It continues to be cold. Absolutely frigid this morning. A thick frost covered the entire upper deck as well as our ladder between decks. I may not be able to visit my spot on deck today. I may stay in the warmth of my blankets as long as possible. There is no real reason to get up, except Elder Brewster will expect us all at services this morning. It is Sunday, so other than that I will rest for the day. There is no child to take care of. William is independent and fully capable of caring for himself. There are no errands to run. No house to tidy. If we were back home, I would be looking out the front window at the frost. I would be sitting by the fire, warm and toasty, and deciding when or even whether to go out in the cold. Here, there is no choice. There is no warm fire. We will endure another cold day and hope the sun comes out strong by midday.

Bless the Lord, O my soul. O Lord my God, thou art very great; thou art clothed with honour and majesty.

Who coverest thyself with light as with a garment: who stretchest out the heavens like a curtain:

Who layeth the beams of his chambers in the waters: who maketh the clouds his chariot: who walketh upon the wings of the wind:
— Psalm 104:1–3

Priscilla was kind enough to bring me a warm mug of ginger tea, which motivated me to get out of bed this morning. Elder Brewster's encouraging words from God's gracious gift of the Psalms made me quite ashamed of starting my day with a whiny attitude. And once the sun did come out, it was a beautiful day.

It occurred to me why we had a strong frost during the night. There was no cloud cover. I know this because as I was getting into bed last night, I looked out the small peephole closest to our bunk and saw the moon hanging low in the sky, delicately balanced as if dangling by a thread, near the western horizon. Not quite a quarter moon, I could easily make out the clear, crisp pointed tips on both her topside and bottom. I truly can't think of anything prettier in all of God's creation than that beautiful light that shines out in the darkest of nights. What a glorious idea to place a gift in the black night sky. What a marvel that our Creator of Earth and Heaven thought to send us that small encouragement. Light when all around us is dark. True, we had to endure a thick morning frost because of it, but the sight of that beautiful light in the sky last night was well worth it.

Monday, October 23

Jesus answered, Verily, verily, I say unto thee, Except a man be born of water and of the Spirit, he cannot enter into the kingdom of God.
— John 3:5

Dear Jaqueline,

The sailor who was baptized last week is named John. There must be over a dozen men on this ship with that glorious name.

William has taken a particular interest in this John and meets with him night after night, going over various passages from the Bible. John serves double duty as both a member of the crew and the guardian of our food and drink in the hold. Last night he was able to guard the entrance to the hold and listen to Elder Brewster's sermon to us from 1 Peter. It was an encouraging message for me, but we suspected that hearing it for the first time might create some questions for this newest believer, and it rightly did.

"Ye also, as lively stones, are built up a spiritual house, an holy priesthood, to offer up spiritual sacrifices, acceptable to God by Jesus Christ" (1 Peter 2:5). How am I a living stone? Before the Savior's touch, we are all lifeless, not completely able to understand God's direction or recognize his mighty hand at work in our daily circumstances and situations. We are hardened, following our own plans, but once we claim him as our Savior, we are brought to life to serve and follow the path he opens before us.

"But ye are a chosen generation, a royal priesthood, an holy nation, a peculiar people; that ye should shew forth the praises of him who hath called you out of darkness into his marvellous light" (1 Peter 2:9). How can I be royalty? I don't feel like royalty. I have a past and have done some things that you wouldn't exactly call royal behavior. By believing that Jesus is the Christ, we at once receive his royal blood, which pulses through our veins. In his eyes we are like royalty. It is an amazing love.

"Behold, I lay in Sion a chief corner stone, elect, precious: and he that believeth on him shall not be confounded" (1 Peter 2:6). Christ the cornerstone. When William got to this part of the passage, it was like watching a lamp fill the room with light. As one who works day and night in the hull of the ship, this word picture brought visible peace to John's face and all his questions to an end. While others admire the sails and the mass of a ship above water, John is mostly interested in knowing the details about the hull of the boat. The hull is the foundation, the most important part of the vessel. If not designed properly, it won't carry the full weight of the ship. The hull has to be durable and safe and built in a way that the buoyancy is fixed halfway between the bow and the stern.

Isn't it amazing, how even hundreds of years after Jesus first used those word pictures, that they now bring one simple sailor to a complete and full understanding of the importance of having Christ as the firm foundation for his personal life? What an awesome God we serve!

Thursday, October 26

The Lord is my shepherd; I shall not want.
He maketh me to lie down in green pastures: he leadeth me beside the still waters.
He restoreth my soul: he leadeth me in the paths of righteousness for his name's sake.
— Psalm 23:1–3

Dear Jaqueline,

It has rained almost the entire day, a cold autumn drizzle falling all day long from a gloomy gray sky. At times the wind came whipping down the ladder and marched briskly from one end of our between deck to the other. I'm not feeling well today, so the weather only encouraged me to stay under the covers and let life drift by for a while.

Not much to enjoy in this day. Provisions are down to a minimum. We are running out of firewood and reaching the bottom of the water casks, and we've drunk down to one barrel of beer. Rationing begins. It's odd, but the lack of food serves to increase my thoughts about food. What I would give right now to sample a plum or a pear or a handful of cherries. Then a sip of ginger tea and two spiced cookies. Maybe finish up with a savory tart, a sweet pastry, or a slice of warm rye bread with Momma's delicious jam. And the daydreams go on.

Richard Clarke and Crackstone are starting to show signs of scurvy. At first they complained of feeling weak, almost lethargic. But Dr. Fuller confirmed it was scurvy when he saw their bleeding gums and loosening teeth. Plus, they reportedly have that awful, foul-smelling breath. It's most disgusting and a bit frightening, to be honest.

I am thankful that I have only an upset stomach to deal with. My biggest problem seems to come from food I'm not accustomed to eating. Don't get me wrong, I am thankful, thankful, thankful for getting a daily portion. It's that sometimes it does not settle well with my stomach and leads to a complete day of inactivity.

Even though I'm not feeling well enough to help with daily chores, I'm determined to make the most of this quiet rest. Do you think God provides days of rest for a reason? I pray that if that's the case that I hear all he intends me to hear. My ears and mind are wide open. Maybe he's preparing me for what lies ahead.

From my bunk I can see Aunt Susanna's little boy running up and down the middle aisle. He is almost five now and reminds me of little John on those days when he could be a giant bundle of energy, capable of pumping gallons of activity and adventure into the tiniest of play spaces. I say a prayer for you and Momma to be equipped and prepared for the challenges that lie ahead with him this winter. I know on any rainy day when he's cooped up that his energy level can be hard to deal with. I pray that you will have strength and spirit to keep up with him. I pray that he will behave well for you and especially hope he doesn't get sick like last winter. That fever came out of nowhere; it was so odd and scary, and then it disappeared as suddenly as it arrived.

Speaking of fever, I would ask your prayers for renewed health for Butten. It's puzzling. I know God answers prayers. I know God has the power to heal Butten completely. Every single day I am praying for Butten to be healed. But instead of seeing him gain strength, we are seeing a slow and steady decline. Mary Brewster and I take turns sitting with him daily because he is barely able to get out of bed. It seems to lift his spirits in some small way. We talk about traveling. We talk about things he remembers from Leiden. Sometimes he doesn't want to talk and looks deep in thought as if he's having a conversation with someone who's not even here. It makes me wonder if the true healing he needs is for something not physical. Perhaps there's some issue from his past that requires a healing in his mind. Perhaps there's some deep, personal part of him that needs healing. I want to know, but sometimes these things are only between a person and their God. I will continue to trust God and pray for his healing, even though there may be no visible sign of it at all.

Saturday, October 28

Every good gift and every perfect gift is from above, and cometh down from the Father of lights, with whom is no variableness, neither shadow of turning.
— James 1:17

Dear Jaqueline,

It's now day three of rain. We get short reprieves, but then the sky will open, and again it pours. It's a perfect day to lie here and write to you.

I enjoy watching William speak to the men; he has a true gift for leading. There's something in his tone that commands authority and gives him a strange ability to bring calmness to a scene of utter chaos. It's not a gift I have. Sometimes, in fact, I find myself speaking and wonder if others are even listening to my words. At times my speaking seems to give others pause for introspection, and instead of listening to my words, their eyes glaze over, and they appear to drift off into thoughts of their own, maybe sorting out the details of the topic. I'm never sure. I can sometimes be bold with my words, but I don't have the knack of commanding the conversation in the manner he does.

So, it amazes me. Why would one so talented, one so skilled at leading, choose me as his companion? What did he see in me? Why did I win his heart? It wasn't my ability to persuade, as I feel inadequate in that area. What was it in me that stood out to him? I know it was God who brought us together and directed our circumstances to find one another.

I can still remember the first time I heard about William. Our sweet friend Martha came back from her appointment at the fabric shop. She was all excited about a young man's wisdom and skill in fabric. She went on and on about his handiwork, his handsome looks, and his smile so kind.

Then one day, without notice, he showed up at laundry day to help us carry the large loads. And then it became a regular occurrence. I clearly remember the day he turned directly to me and asked why I was thinking of starting a fabric store of my own. I stopped in my tracks and laughed, responding with, "Where did you ever get an idea like that?" I spoke clearly and confidently, although I don't know how, and told him I had no intention of starting my own shop. That somehow led him to telling me all about his intentions to open his own store. We talked on and on, and before I knew it, he had shared the real story of losing his mother and father and the struggles that led him to find the Brewsters and Pastor Robinson's congregation. And then I remember thinking, "Why are you telling me all these details of your life?" and wondering if it were me he wanted to get to know better, me he wanted to share his life with. Still so amazing to me.

Funny that now, seven years later, he still makes my heart skip a beat. I wish you could have seen him speaking today. When he spoke, they were captivated. They absorbed his conviction and strength. It's different from when Elder Brewster leads our worship. Elder Brewster is an amazing worship leader. He is Spirit-led, and we all feel the presence of God in our worship. But with William's gifts, I am convinced God has a special role for him in all of this; I'm anxious to see what it is.

It makes me wonder whether little John has inherited William's natural gift of speaking. I remember the day little John was born. I went to pick him up from the cradle and gasped to myself at how much he looked like me. All his facial features—cheeks, nose, eyes, even the way his mouth curved slightly downward—the resemblance to me was startling, like I was looking at a reflection of myself in a mirror. It was truly a surreal moment. But now he looks more and more like William and is beginning more and more to act like his father.

Will he be more inclined to speak about facts or his emotions? More inclined to speak his mind or wait for the right question to be asked? I can be quite comfortable in a large group setting, and with God's help I have learned to find words when I need to speak my mind, but inside I am always a bit timid when it comes to large groups. I am much more comfortable in one-on-one conversations with people I'm accustomed to.

William knows no stranger. William sees a public gathering as a platform to share, present, and test his ideas. He seems to perceive the public reaction and then continues to develop his thought based on how that public reacted. I, on the other hand, don't seem so concerned about public reaction and would rather base my thoughts on my convictions. I know I get that from Poppa and Momma. I wonder where William learned his ability to speak so confidently. Were his parents like that? We have no way of knowing, no ability to trace these traits back to anyone in his family.

And where did he get that thirst for learning? He knows Latin and Greek and now Dutch and Hebrew, and most of that was self-taught. Already I see in little John a similar thirst for learning, which I know you and Momma will encourage. There's the benefit of a loving family. Poor William never had that. Well, he did for those early years, and he was able to stay with family after his father and mother died. But little John has not only William and me but you and Momma and an entire community of strong believers who surround and support him. Compare that to William, who grew up rather isolated in the small village of Austerfield and was almost an adult before he ventured out. Little John will travel halfway around the world to live in a new country before he reaches the age of five. Talk about an education! It will be interesting to see how all this affects his development in the growing years and how God molds and shapes the personality of that beautiful boy.

Sunday, October 29

O Lord, our Lord, how excellent is thy name in all the earth! who hast set thy glory above the heavens...
When I consider thy heavens, the work of thy fingers, the moon and the stars, which thou hast ordained.
— Psalm 8:1, 3

Dear Jaqueline,

This evening we have a full moon on the horizon. Or almost a full moon. It's missing a smidge of the full circle. And I don't know what made tonight's view different, but it was amazing. I'm not sure how to explain it, but normally when I look up at the moon, it seems flat against the night sky. Tonight it was as if we were seeing the whole globe. It was somehow dimensional, like we could see the full round ball, suspended in midair. It was the oddest sensation. It was like looking into the depth of the night sky, behind the moon, extending into never-ending space.

I've always been a bit puzzled by how the moon can reflect the light of the sun. It doesn't make sense to my nonscientific brain. But I know that God makes it happen. William says it's like when Jesus lives in us and we reflect his light to others. We're not sure exactly how that happens, but we know God makes it happen. I wish I understood it all better.

This is the second full moon we've had this month, and our ship is driving straight into its illuminating orange glow. William and I should have climbed into bed like all the others, but I begged him to stay on deck. It was an amazing scene of complete peace and pure beauty. Moonlight reflected off the calm, quiet water. A cool, fresh breeze filled the night air with promise. And in the stillness we praised God for our safe travels, for our healthy minds and bodies and spirits. We prayed for peace among the passengers. It was quite a contrast to the stagnant smells and darkness below. You know, if I could have, I would have persuaded him to sleep up there all night.

Tuesday, October 31

Nevertheless I am continually with thee: thou has holden me by my right hand. Thou shalt guide me with thy counsel, and afterword receive me to glory.
— Psalm 73:23-24

Unto thee, O God, do we give thanks, unto thee do we give thanks: for that thy name is near thy wondrous works declare.
— Psalm 75:1

Thy way, O God, is in the sanctuary: who is so great a God as our God?
— Psalm 77:13

Turn us again, O Lord God of hosts, cause thy face to shine; and we shall be saved.
— Psalm 80:19

That men may know that thou, whose name alone is Jehovah, art the most high over all the earth.
— Psalm 83:18

Dear Jaqueline,

Not only is it frigid cold, but this morning we had snow on the upper deck—not much, but enough to complain about. Every step of the ladder was coated with an icy, slushy white snow, making it unfit to climb to my spot.

Once again, I am huddled under blankets, and in doing so I have received a great peace from reading the Psalms of Asaph. It was a broken world in his time, just as it is a broken world in my time. Even he, so many years ago, described a world that was falling apart, where evil was affecting all around him and oppression had a foothold.

A few months ago it seemed that war was right around the corner.[19] But reading these verses today brings a peace for which I am eternally grateful. It's the kind of peace that makes no sense. It goes beyond understanding. It's a calmness that comes over me, and I think it is visible too. That peace reminds me of the days when I was little. Momma always said I behaved like I had no worries. Was I supposed to have worries in those growing years? She and Poppa took care of everything. If I did have a worry, she was the one I turned to. And gradually God became my refuge and my strength, the one I went to with my worries. Today, while the world around me looks like it is falling apart, I talk to him. He is my refuge. He is all I need.

Wednesday, November 1

Trust in the Lord, and do good; so shalt thou dwell in the land, and verily thou shalt be fed.
Delight thyself also in the Lord; and he shall give thee the desires of thine heart.
Commit thy way unto the Lord; trust also in him; and he shall bring it to pass.
— Psalm 37:3–5

Dear Jaqueline,

There's something so peaceful about an early morning sky. The sun is not up yet, but there is enough light for everything now to be visible. The moon has set. The stars have gone into hiding. We have another deep frost, and there are low clouds on the horizon, light cream and gray, stretching from one edge to another. Again, nothing but water and sky everywhere I look. No land in sight. No trees. Nothing but sky and water pouring, one into the other, in every direction. But the sky is this beautiful shade of blue.

How can one describe a shade of blue? I don't remember seeing a flower this color. It's like a baby-blue hat or blanket. Soft, gentle, pure. I think the sky's blue is different from any other color because it's not a flat color painted on a paper. It's a deep dimensional color, so all the shades and layers reflect back to me. It's a rich baby blue. I'd like to paint this color but am not very gifted at painting. I wish I could share this view with you and little John. Even when he comes with you, I won't be able to share this sense of sky and water with him. But maybe knowing my experience of it may encourage him to look for it when you make your own travels here. I will encourage you to seek it when he comes.

I think way too much about him. I worry sometimes that I think about him more than a mother should. Maybe more than I think about my God. I'll see something in my day and think of him. Someone will laugh funny, and I'll think of him. One of the children will say something, and I'll think of him. Maybe that's normal for a mother. I should talk to Mary about it and see what she thinks.

Monday, November 6

Jesus said unto her, I am the resurrection, and the life: he that believeth in me, though he were dead, yet shall he live:
And whosoever liveth and believeth in me shall never die. Believest thou this?
— John 11:25–26

Dear Jaqueline,

I have been sitting here this morning for the longest time. Just sitting. Holding my head in my hands. Unable to process. Unable to make sense of what has happened in these last few days. Not sure if I am ready to face the reality of it. It all seems completely surreal.

We've been taking care of Butten for several days. He's been sick with a terrible cough. He became completely bedridden on Friday, and the cough started keeping him awake at night, so Dr. Fuller arranged a twenty-four-hour watch to make sure he stayed comfortable.

We've had a reprieve from the cold, which I am oh so thankful for. At times what seemed like a warm spring breeze flowed from one end of the be-tween deck to the other, bringing a spirit of hopefulness to all. Even during my shift with Butten yesterday afternoon, it looked like the medicine was fi-nally helping him. We joked a little, and he ate a little. He seemed to be a slight bit stronger, and his cough seemed to be a little less worrisome. But through-out the afternoon he would say things as if he knew he was dying, things like the name of a psalm he would like to have sung at his funeral and verses he would like Elder Brewster to read. I didn't say much but kept thinking to my-self, "Why are you telling me these things when you are starting to get better?" I literally did not grasp what was happening before my very eyes.

Mary woke me in the darkest hour of the night. She nudged my arm and held her finger to her lips and motioned at me to stay quiet. I slipped out of the bunk and followed her to Butten's cot and knew immediately something was wrong. Often, we took little notice of his cries, but these sounds were different. His head was burning hot, so we grabbed fresh cloths and took turns with cool water to try and bring the fever down. We woke Dr. Fuller, who seemed immediately to know that the situation was worsening.

From then on it all got confusing. Sometimes Butten spoke to us with clarity, and I thought to myself, "He's going to pull out of this. He's going to be fine." It seemed difficult for him to talk, so we encouraged him to rest and lie still. During one long stretch he was so quiet that Mary even mentioned going to lie down for a while so she could be refreshed for the daybreak shift. Thank God she decided to stay. At one point he said he was feeling quite strange. I think back on that now and wonder why I didn't ask him more about that. What did he mean? I simply did not understand that he was slipping away. I think Dr. Fuller knew, but he has seen death approach many times. I have only seen it this close once or twice and did not recognize or sense its presence. I think Butten knew exactly what was happening. He was courageous and strong and steady, at one point clearly whispering to us, "Please tell my young friend Samuel that I died with a smile on my face."

I remember thinking, "God, please don't let him die now; we are so close to our destination. Can't he stay alive a few more days so we can get him off this awful ship?" But God had a different plan. A pale quarter moon was barely visible through the porthole. It peeked in and out of thin clouds and brought the smallest amount of light to his face. He looked so peaceful. Mary and I each grabbed his hands and kept telling him that everything was going to be all right, but there in that soft morning moonlight he took his last breath, slipped away, and was gone from us.

It is not easy to witness anyone's passing from life to death, the sacred moment as they cross the thin line between this life and the next. For his sake I am so thankful that we were able to be beside him, to comfort him and tell him of God's love, to remind him of God's forgiveness, and to make sure he knew he was in a safe place. I never would have wanted that poor young man to die alone. He had been abandoned by so many, and we did not abandon him in that final hour. For his sake I am grateful that others all around were sleeping and unaware. It was a private moment for us.

Dr. Fuller slipped away and went to notify Elder Brewster. Master Jones came silently down the ladder, and the three men carried Butten to the deck before the light of day.

I have no idea what to do until the day begins except write my thoughts to you, Jaqueline. I can tell you that the scenes, the conversations, and the images are playing over and over and over in my mind, and I can't stop thinking about his death. On one hand I have a complete sense of peace about the way these circumstances fell into place over the last few days: the hour of the day when all were sleeping, the peacefulness of his passing, God's very presence there with us. It is beyond precious that the three of us were there to help him in his final moments and comfort him as best we could. I may always wonder whether we should have done something differently. Should we have awakened the elders for group prayer? Should we have moved Butten upstairs for fresh air? I don't even know. I am struggling to think clearly, but what I find even more puzzling was my state of mind that must have been in complete denial of what was happening. Dr. Fuller knew exactly what was happening. Butten knew exactly what was going on. And he had no fear. He was a perfect picture of calmness and peace, as if a steady light were guiding him through any darkness or confusion of the moment, leading him into a peaceful Kingdom with Jesus. I can't quite convince myself that he's gone.

The morning sky begins to color and light with a thousand shades of pink and gray. Tones stretch from one edge of the eastern horizon to the other, not a pale pink but a more brilliant shade, somewhere between pink and red; it's hard to pin down exactly what hue it is. It's not a comforting quiet whisper of a color but a bold, stark statement arching out from the horizon. Slowly, intently, the colors and clouds spread, growing in intensity until the entire sky is ablaze with pink, as if washing the sky with a brilliant announcement, awakening all my senses to the very presence of the day. It is a stunning and powerful reminder that death holds no sting, that the same power that raised Christ from the dead is living in us! Praise be to God!

With eyes on our heavenly home this will still be difficult to bear. I dread sharing this news with others, especially William, especially his young friend Samuel. But I have no choice but to head straight into the grief as if heading straight into a dark storm cloud. That receding moon is still visible straight overhead. It is a comfort to know that the heavenly hosts have shared this experience of the last few hours with me. I wish you were here to share this burden as well.

Wednesday, November 8

But now thus saith the Lord that created thee, O Jacob, and he that formed thee, O Israel, Fear not: for I have redeemed thee, I have called thee by thy name; thou art mine.

When thou passest through the water, I will be with thee; and through the rivers, they shall not overflow thee: when thou walkest through the fire, thou shalt not be burned: neither shall the flame kindle upon thee.
— Isaiah 43:1–2

Dear Jaqueline,

We must be getting closer to land; there have been multiple porpoise sightings over the last couple days. Sometimes a group of two or three. Sometimes as many as ten to twenty in their group. Are they here to cheer us on as we approach the finish line? One can only hope. We have no way of knowing. Gulls are seen more often, roaming the sky above. The seas are thankfully calm, but these last couple days have been exhausting.

Normally I would recognize this lack of strength as an accompanying symptom of grief, but there seems more to this. Unanswered questions and doubts weigh heavy on us now. Was Butten the first of many who will lose strength and will? Will death overtake us all before the journey's end? Will this ghastly journey ever reach an end?

Elder Brewster is doing his best to keep us encouraged, but the passing of Butten has left many drained of energy and hope, with little to renew. Children whine throughout the entire day. Lessons have been stopped for the time. We are running out of food because our voyage has taken much longer than planned. Is this our low point?

I am sad for all the children on this journey who have to experience death in these close quarters. The presence of death is most unwelcome. I am especially sad for Dr. Fuller. He tried everything imaginable to save that boy. He has already lost a child and his first wife. He is most lonely now for his second wife and child who stayed behind in Leiden, and he has no choice but to make the rest of the journey without Butten, a dear and faithful companion.

I am oh so grateful for my short-lived friendship with Butten and the opportunities I had to get to know him on this journey. It is strange indeed to have no family to contact about this news of his death. William, Elder Brewster, and Dr. Fuller made plans for a memorial of sorts when we reach shore. I hope to find a shell and place it with his marker as a statement that he made it safely to shore, to his eternal home. I also have his sailing cap, one of his only family treasures, from his grandfather, I think. I don't know yet whether to place it in the memorial or keep it in a special place in our home as a remembrance of his courage.

I can't seem to shake myself of the whole experience yet. Last night I had odd dreams. In one I was walking, holding on to bars of some kind, on both sides of me, but I was up to my knees in this dark, murky water. Every step was a challenge to lift my foot out of the muddy, sandy bottom. And with every step the water all around my legs filled with a million particles of mud and sand and dirt. I was not afraid but kept moving forward one step at a time. Later in that dream, or maybe it was in a separate dream, I was crossing a sandbar in what appeared to be a rapidly flowing river. Maybe it wasn't a river exactly, but more like a wide section of a brook or stream. The water was clean and swift. There were eddies, small swirling pools, currents full of energy and rushing water. There were large rocks and trees on either side. It was a beautiful scene, full of life and absolutely no sense of danger. Is God trying to teach me something?

Even though part of me was in denial in those hours when Butten passed from life to death, I had several moments of pure courage and strength that gave me the smallest ledge to cling to. Watching him in the soft moonlight reminded me that our time on this miserable ship is not just about our passage to America but more importantly about our passage to our heavenly home. There we were, Mary and I, witnessing the temporal giving way to the eternal. Butten passed from this life into an experience far better than we could ever imagine, departing this great darkness to enter an eternally brilliant light.

Mary says she was strengthened during those hours as well. I am so thankful we were together during that time. It is good to have a friend who went through the entire experience with me. There is a shared understanding, a new tie that binds us now. I am so glad Butten is no longer bound by his pain and sickness and am so proud of his valiant fight. I am thankful he is living in the glorious light of God's goodness now but sad he is no longer here with us. I miss his quirky smile and funny sense of humor. I have lost a true friend and truly look forward to seeing him in heaven one day.

Thursday, November 9

Ask, and it shall be given you; seek, and ye shall find; knock, and it shall be opened unto you:
For everyone that asketh receiveth; and he that seeketh findeth; and to him that knocketh it shall be opened.
— Matthew 7:7–8

Jaqueline,

Was it just yesterday I mentioned our desperate need of encouragement? Today God has answered, and we are blessed with hope and inexpressible gratefulness. It was after daybreak. William and I were rinsing bowls from the morning meal, and the word rang out. That precious, sweet word we've been waiting for, anticipating, dreaming of hearing, hoping to hear. Who knew the power of that word? "Land!"

We both dropped our bowls, grabbed hands, and raced up the ladder. Shouts broke out! We hugged, laughed, sang praises to our God! Everything was a sudden flurry of chaos as we contended for a spot to see. And then there it was. We could barely make out the thin black edge stretched out along the horizon, extending far, far to the south and all the way to the north, as far as we could see.

The early morning sun was coming up behind us, and dazzling light played tricks on the water, making the stretch of dark land hard to keep in focus. In fact, at times I questioned whether it was real. Perhaps the crew was mistaken and instead it was only a long low-lying cloud. But as those first few minutes went on, the expanse of land grew firm before our eyes. A late quarter moon was still visible straight overhead. What a beautiful sight!

At one point I looked for Aunt Susanna and realized she might need help coming up from below. I found her in the main cabin with Katherine Carver and young Dorothy excitedly telling her all that was taking place up above. Aunt Susanna's ankles have greatly swollen in these last few days, so she had not even attempted to make it up the ladder. I ran up for William, and he quickly organized a group of men. They gently helped Aunt Susanna and then Mary Allerton, who needed help as well, to a spot on the upper deck where they were safely able to draw in the fresh air and amazing sight of land. What an encouragement this is for all of us.

Master Jones appeared from the cabin and confirmed the crew's report.

A celebration atmosphere continued all morning. Families hugged, neighbors hugged, strangers hugged. The joy was contagious. Crew members shouted and sang. Children ran about. Every difficulty we have faced in our days of travel—loss, sickness, storms, terror, hunger, hardships—all of it seems behind us now. Burdens and trials are forgotten for the moment. Even those not feeling well were brought up from below and were lifted in spirit.

It is a most joyous time and a humbling experience. We needed this boost. We needed it today. Once again, God is perfect in his timing. To lay eyes on that beautiful stretch of sandy beach was to commit all over again to the promise and the purpose of why we are here. God has indeed proven faithful and seen us safely across the great waters. Sixty-four long and treacherous days on the sea; sixty-four long days in cramped, dark quarters together; sixty-four long days of trials and sickness and loss. My thoughts wander back to all the hopes and plans and dreams, to the days of early meetings in Pastor Robinson's house, and now here we are with the reality of our new home stretching before us.

Has our journey come to an end? Or is our journey just now beginning? We all know that it will be a few more days before we feel that solid, sandy ground beneath our feet. For the moment, we are in sight of it, and that is all that matters. Elder Brewster gathered us on the deck and led a prayer of thanks. I couldn't help but notice the contrast of that filthy deck we knelt on and that beautiful stretch of land that brings new hope.

But if we hope for that we see not, then do we with patience wait for it.
— Romans 8:25

Somehow we returned to morning chores, but within a couple of hours Master Jones reported to the men that the land-mass growing in the west is actually a long arm called the Cape.[20] He has studied the land and maps from his cabin and is convinced we are well out of range of our targeted destination, far to the north of it. Apparently that last storm threw us off course more than two hundred miles. The men are alarmed and furious.

Master Jones, being sensitive to our weakening health, is pushing to get us to shore by the fastest route. Apparently, there are advantages to settling in this Cape, well known for its fisheries. But the men gave no room for debate. They are insistent we must land where we have legally been granted land. God forbid that we would upset the King—he let us go to establish this settlement, and the last thing we want to do is upset him. Master Jones then admitted that the winds are in favor of heading south, so we will make our way to the Hudson..

And hope maketh not ashamed; because the love of God is shed abroad in our hearts by the Holy Ghost which is given unto us.
— Romans 5:5

The air is chilly, but I determined to stay on deck most of the afternoon in the sun, praying it keeps all sickness at bay. The ship moves easily as we follow the shoreline. We are out of the high sea winds and closing in on our homeland, Jaqueline. It is indeed an amazing respite. I am most anxious for you to receive this good news of the day. I wish Butten had lived a few more days. The sight of this beautiful stretch of land might have encouraged him.

Friday, November 10

Because thou hast made the Lord, which is my refuge, even the most High,
thy habitation;
There shall no evil befall thee, neither shall any plague come nigh thy dwelling.
For he shall give his angels charge over thee, to keep thee in all thy ways.
They shall bear thee up in their hands, lest thou dash thy foot against a stone.
— Psalm 91:9–12

Dear Jaqueline,

Our decision yesterday to follow the coast south to the Hudson led to more trauma than I care to write about. Suffice it to say we are exhausted from the peril of the journey.

For several hours we moved along at a peaceful clip, grateful to be finally closing in on our destination, excitedly anticipating new beginnings. Seeing how no one on board had maps to guide us from the Cape to the Hudson, we had no idea that a stretch of hell itself lay between us and our longed-for Hudson River.[21] All I remember now is how quickly we entered calamity and how a matter of minutes shifted our emotions from excited anticipation to full-fledged fear. Like a startling slap in the face, the tide turned, and we scrambled for safety. Huge waves first crashed in from the east, tipping us westward and throwing us toward the shore. Responding waves tossed us back. Back and forth we were trapped as dangerous crests pounded our *Mayflower* throughout the afternoon.

The crew was as frustrated as I've seen them, unable to find stability in the massive waves and unable to back out, like a nightmare we couldn't wake from. Poor Master Jones was in a quandary. On one hand he faced a frightening mob of disgruntled men, all fearing for their lives if the ship landed anywhere but where the King provided; on the other, he was chartering a boat full of weakened, sick passengers and was unable to find a way around the brutal, vicious, unending churn. Some encouraged him to anchor and ride out the crest, but I'm sure we would not have survived the night. Just before dusk, the wind shifted slightly, and the crew was finally able to pull free from the tumultuous waters. Once again, at the mercy of God, we have only him to thank for rescue. "God has spoken," William whispered to me. Master Jones decided to return to the Cape. Dark came quickly, and once the ship was outside of the rough water, we dropped anchor.

That's when the real uproar started. As William explained it to me, heading back to the Cape puts our life in danger because our patent is procured for Virginia, not New England. But there is no way to get to the Hudson. Through most of the night and most of today, men have stepped forward and shared their minds and deepest fears before all.

The worry and concern have taken their toll on all. But there is no turning back now. By nightfall we will be in the Cape. You know it is often difficult for me when "the plan" changes. The uproar and concerns created a physical tension in my neck and shoulders. I tried to lie down but couldn't get comfortable. I tried to breathe deeply but had to pace up and down our middle aisle. It took me a good two hours before I was able to breathe normally again.

The future of our settlement is now in great peril. Most are physically exhausted and hardly able to think clearly.

Saturday, November 11

*And we know that all things work together for good to them that love God,
to them who are the called according to his purpose.*
— Romans 8:28

Dear Jaqueline,

We are anchored and safe within the harbor. I awakened to the oddest
sensation. It was a steady, slight, rocking motion. It was then I realized—gone
are the large rolling waves and the ferocious winds. And it is quiet all around.
I listen for the harsh words and angry voices of last night, but that storm must
have passed as well.

I stayed awake late into the night listening to Mullins and Martin arguing
that the only way for us to financially meet the demands upon us is for everyone to work together. William was here beside me when I awoke but says he
didn't sleep a wink. He tells me that not long after I fell asleep someone sug-
gested drafting a contract, a written pledge to one another, a document that
would declare our full submission to the group as its own entity and promise
our obedience to the group.

He said it was funny listening to the idea unfold and then formulate into
a full-fledged plan; each man had a chance to weigh in, and in the end each
man nodded in agreement. It was such a simple idea, and yet it seemed to
satisfy every concern and doubt that had been raised throughout the evening.
It was proposed as an agreement that will provide legitimacy to our colony
and allow us to establish right here where we are. It's a godsend—that's what
I call it—an amazing solution., He says that several men stayed up through
the night to draft the document.[22]

At the first sign of daylight all our able-bodied men gathered in the ship's
great cabin. Spirits were high, even to the point of excitement. All eligible
men signed the new deed. Then they voted Carver to be governor for the first
year. I am doubly thankful for that—a just and honest man. He will be a trust-
worthy official.

While the men were busy in the cabin, Mary and I and several other
women took the children up on deck to look around. It was the most eerie feeling, Jaqueline—finally arriving, but not only are we the only ship in the harbor,
there are no homes, no people, not a sign of civilization anywhere.

It is definitely not Virginia. It is definitely not what we expected to find.
There are trees, trees, and more trees in every direction we look. But they

have lost all their leaves. Even though it's only November, it has the look and feel of winter here. Tall trunks and barren branches like paint brushes of various sizes and shapes point to the sky, poised as if ready to be selected for the Creator's next masterpiece on a blue-sky canvas. It's odd to think that we had nothing but water and sky for days and days and days, and now we have nothing but stark, barren wilderness for miles and miles and miles.

Once the document was signed, the men came bustling out of the cabin, revitalized and making plans for the day ahead. There is much to be done; it's difficult to know exactly where to start. William is working with Browne and Goodman to outline plans for exploration. John Alden and several others are assigned to organize and document all our remaining supplies. Carver and Standish are in charge of setting nets and traps for fishing. The women and children were starting down the ladder to fix our morning meal, but Elder Brewster spoke up. It brought a hush to our entire group. I can't remember his exact words, but it was something like this:

"Tomorrow is our Lord's Day, our first full opportunity to worship since arriving here safely. While I know there is much to be done and that you are anxious to start our plans, there may not be a more fitting day to fall on our knees and worship the One who got us here safely, the One who blessed our journey and has perfect plans for our days here in the new country. Yes, there is much to be done, but I plead with you—let's set aside tomorrow to thank God for all he's provided. Let us present each of our specific requests before him. It's his work we are here to do. We've traveled a wild and vast ocean in search of a place where we can freely worship. So, let us begin tomorrow. My friends, this is the core of who we are, and for this reason—our freedom of worship—we've come. Let us not lose sight of that and get carried away by our task list. As important as each task is, I firmly believe that our day spent in worship of the Lord will do more to guide us, to encourage us, to make our path straight, than any of these plans we're speaking of. Let us finish making these plans today and then set them aside. We will lift each plan in prayer tomorrow and ask that God bless each step. Let us give our God all the praise and blessing and honor he so richly deserves."

Perhaps it was the humbling tone in his speech. Or maybe the perfect timing for his words. Of course this is not about building homes or finding the perfect place to settle. Of course we should dedicate all that we're about to do to our God. Some will think it's not productive, because there's much work to be done. It is our human tendency to immediately start the work. Find food. Gather materials for building. The harsh winter is right around the corner. We cannot waste a minute. The crew is anxious to get us off the ship so they can return to England before winter sets in. But skip our day of worship? There may be some who are thinking that God will understand because he knows how much work is before us. But funny—no one voiced an objection. If someone disagrees, they are keeping it to themselves. Elder Brewster is right. If any day deserves to be set aside for worship, it is our first Sunday in this new land. God has safely seen us across the vast ocean. He deserves our hearts, minds, and bodies and all our praises for the entire day and more. I am convinced this will set our course, hearts, and minds right for all the work ahead.

Sunday, November 12

Fear not, little flock; for it is your Father's good pleasure to give you the kingdom.
— Luke 12:32

Dear Jaqueline,

Although we are anxious to get our feet on solid ground, it was only appropriate that we spent the entire day in prayer and worship. And what a day of rejoicing it was! Elder Brewster led worship this morning, and we are resting now.

Don't you think it's funny that the Lord saw to it that our first full day here would be a day of worship? I love the Lord's plan! It's so like him to time our arrival like this. Would we have taken a full day of rest and worship to celebrate if today was any other day but Sunday? Knowing this group, we would have had a prayer and then jumped right in to all that needs to be done. Instead, we are taking the day to dedicate our work, our bodies, and our hearts to carry out the Lord's plan. Not our plan, but God's. Instead, we are taking time to express deep gratitude and thanks for his saving grace, for our safe arrival here, and for our names in his book of eternity. We are taking the day to fully understand what it means to rest in his arms.

This morning the bay was calm, and having the boat secure in a harbor made a big difference in our worship time. It made me realize how stressful our times of worship were out on the open sea, with the constant rocking and interruptions of crashing waves, blowing sails, and busy sailors hard at work keeping the boat moving. We did our best in those circumstances, but here no massive waves crash over the deck or pour down through the deck cracks. We've had an entire morning without seasickness. Today's worship was filled with a quiet and peace and tranquility that we haven't experienced for months. We soaked in the true meaning of God's calming power and presence, a complete sense of security.

We were blessed with a sunny day and we gathered on the main deck. The sun warmed us. Birds sang and flew overhead. I can't even find the words to describe the blue of the sky. The closest thing I can come up with is the blue of the precious healing lapis stone. Deep celestial blue. The blue of royalty and honor. It's as if the sky itself is full of wisdom if only we will listen. And even though our view is an empty, bleak landscape, my thoughts and my eyes were lifted to the sky, lifted from dismay to praise, for God's overwhelming grace.

Master Jones, exhausted from the struggle of the last few days, stayed in his cabin. But many of the crew celebrated with us and joined in singing and prayer. This journey has bound us in our experience. We are survivors. We work together well. Those who had no previous desire to worship sang alongside us and praised along with us, drawn closer to a God who was perhaps distant before this journey began. How interesting that our initial plan was to build our own community where we could raise our families and worship according to God's Word and that already through his providence God is showing us the beauty of outreach to strangers, to the crew. God will yet have his way with those who don't know him.

Nothing seemed important today except singing, praying, and reading from God's Word. I can honestly say I don't remember a worship service so meaningful. Elder Brewster's morning message was about David and Goliath, and our courage and strength were renewed. Like David, he said, we must practice our spiritual fighting skills every day. Be faithful in the little things. Make prayer our way of life. Only then will we be prepared to face God's enemies when the time comes.

Now when we speak of our bleak circumstances, it is not in complaint but in simply lifting them up to our God in prayer. We lifted each worry: concerns for food, concerns for health, concerns for finding a place to build our homes, concerns about building before the weather turns against us. What a relief to let go of each concern, turn it over to God, and acknowledge his perfect plan over each circumstance. Our minds were cleared to focus on the task at hand with reaffirmed purpose and understanding of why we are here, of what we are doing, and of whom we are doing this work for.

The land of promise we planned for, prayed for, dreamed of, and longed for is now right before us. We are indeed here, and this actually must be God's plan for us. It brings a total sense of amazement that he alone saw us safely to this place. He sustains us still.

Great is our God! His mercy endures forever and is new every morning. There is no way we could have made it here without his protective hand. Did I doubt it at times? You know I did. There were days in the deep sea when no sense of direction and nothing but water all around did create inner doubts that we would see our destination.

And here, Jaqueline, I will be completely honest. While that sense of dread from the journey is now unreservedly gone, I can sense it being replaced by new doubts emerging in the corners of my mind. Questions are starting to formulate, and it's tempting to focus on the bleak circumstances all around us. How will we ever accomplish what we are here to do? How will we get along with the unknown inhabitants, the frightening creatures? I look at the shoreline, Jaqueline, and all I see is desolate and unsettled land. Are we surrounded by unseen enemies? I don't know. It's a territory we know nothing about; it's far off course from the land we were registered for. The harshness of winter is coming in fast. We are dealing with health issues and discouragement. Many are missing the families we left behind, including me. We are a hungry, unhealthy group of travelers separated from our country and any help we could call upon there. I don't know what I expected, but at times I find myself saying, "What have we done; what were we thinking?"

Now that we're here, it's as if the journey is just beginning. Getting here has been a major undertaking that I underestimated what it will require to start now, from scratch, and build our homes and our community. May God strengthen me for the work ahead. In my mind I can see buildings and yards and a small community, but I wonder how we will overcome all these obstacles. In my heart I know the only way to get there is the same way we got across that ocean now behind us—one day at a time, one step at a time, following where the Lord leads.

In moments of clarity I can rationalize these doubts. I know they come because I'm tired and weak from a long journey, lack of sleep and lack of proper food. So, all I can do is pray God will equip me to overcome these concerns. Please pray for me too. Pray that in spite of our harsh conditions, God will fill me each day with peace and strength and wisdom for dealing with this chaos. Pray that I will draw courage and confidence from him in the morning hours to carry me through each day. Already I am asking for forgiveness—my mind wanders frequently to plans for tomorrow; I find it difficult to focus. I miss you all so terribly and wish you were here with me to face these challenges.

Monday, November 13

Come unto me, all ye that labour and are heavy laden, and I will give you rest.
Take my yoke upon you, and learn of me; for I am meek and lowly in heart: and ye shall find rest unto your souls.
For my yoke is easy, and my burden is light.
— Matthew 11:28–30

Dear Jaqueline,

I am wrapped tightly in my blanket now, fighting off the evening chill, enjoying space and quiet, which are much needed to reflect on the day. Many are upstairs on deck enjoying a delightful, warm fire. I had no energy to stay with them. Maybe tomorrow I'll have a better outlook.

From here I can barely make out the tiniest sliver of a new moon in the eastern sky. Like a thin white fingernail, it overlooks a vast expanse of blue sky and all that lies below it, including me inside this forsaken ship. Let me go back to the beginning of the day.

I am most grateful for yesterday's day of rest. Without it we may not have made it through the activity of today. We have been months with barely enough activity to keep from getting distraught, and today more energy was required than I had stored. We are exhausted. My head hurts. My legs ache. The entire day has been full of ups and downs. The excitement of having arrived brought joy and cheer, and then it was quickly dimmed by the growing awareness that even once we accomplish a full day of work, we are barely making progress with all that needs to be done. It leads me to feel utterly unstable. One minute I'm fine and the day is bright and sunny. The next I'm a mess and everything is overwhelming.

Immediately after the morning meal, the men and boys vigorously attacked the unpacking of the shallop. It is not in the condition we hoped for. It was quite shocking to see. Though tucked away in a safe spot of the ship and protected with heavy coverings, its four pieces are bruised and battered, splintered and cracked from the hardships of open sea. One look at it and there is no question of why we feel so run-down and worn out. It's been an amazing journey, but it has certainly taken a toll.[23]

Feeling intense pressure now from Master Jones and the crew to clear the main ship, we put an entire team of carpenters to work on the vessel. But their initial report was not good. They now believe the task of assembling requires reconstructing basically from scratch and will take weeks instead of days.

It was just the first of obstacles we are sure to encounter in this New World. There will be no easy way for us here. To settle will require every ounce of fight we have left. We will have to pace ourselves and do the best we can each day.

At one point in the morning I actually thought it delightful to hear their sounds of hammering and sawing. It was a voice of purpose once again. It sounded out a sense of meaning; we are all extremely anxious to find our piece of the work to be done.

After the women and girls rinsed dishes from the morning meal, we set about gathering every piece of filthy, dirty, smelly clothing we could find. As you can imagine, that meant almost every item of clothing we own. From the *Mayflower* to the shallows, the men rowed us to land in Master Jones's smaller boat.

Some were not strong enough to leave the *Mayflower* today—Crackstone, the Martins, Sarah Eaton, Agnes Tilley, Uncle William and the list goes on. There is a contagious infection of some type spreading, and many are now seriously ill. Poor little Jasper has developed a fever, so Katherine Carver was hesitant to leave the ship. John and Alice Rigsdale volunteered to stay behind to take a shift with the sick.

It took three trips to row us to shore. William and I rode over with the second group; a short trip in shallow water is not so scary. I laughed to myself at the thought of capsizing with all that laundry and all those women. What a funny sight that would have been. I was thankful when all were finally safe on shore.

Some of the men grew impatient for their turn; they swam alongside us and then walked the last stretch to shore. Once all were there, some soaking wet and all laughing like a bunch of little children, Elder Brewster gathered us together and led us in the most moving prayer. He offered special prayers for recovery of the sick so they may soon experience this incredible sensation of solid ground. Kneeling together, with land beneath us, was a humbling experience. What an absolute blessing it was to finally set our feet on solid ground, firm and stable earth under our feet. Many could not hold back the tears. I was overwhelmed with a sense of belonging, a sense of home.

Not far from our landing we discovered an amazing pool of fresh water and spent most of the day there bathing, washing and drying clothes, soaking up the sun, and rinsing away the memories of the long, long journey now behind us. Children ran anywhere they found an open space, uphill, downhill, around in circles. We laughed and cried so many times today. Tears of joy. Tears of exhaustion. Tears of utter thankfulness to be finally here.

William and I found a quiet spot not far from the group and we sat there for the greater part of the afternoon breathing in fresh air, not saying much. Just enjoying some time together and listening to the group chatter all around us. We soaked in every sound and every sight of our new land: gentle waves lapping the sands of the bay, gulls diving into the shallows for food. William started working on sketches of our new home. I can picture my house next to the Brewsters or next to the Carvers, but there's no assurance of that. Everyone is anxious to start plans for the settlement and finalize plans for building. What if the final plans have us building next to the Billingtons? Lord help us!

As I sat there, the *Mayflower* bobbed up and down in the bay lazily, like a horse enjoying pasture after running a long race. And the most eerie thought came over me. I realized that I had absolutely no desire to board that ship ever again. There it was, my home for almost three months. You'd think I would have felt more attachment to the ship in that moment. It got us here, and Lord knows I am thankful for the safe journey. But my overwhelming desire at that moment was to never have to set foot on the ship again. When we left this morning, the crew was scrubbing the deck, working to wash off the dirt and grime, but I tell you, Jaqueline, the smell and stench of sickness so permeates our living area that there is no way to get rid of it until we are all completely off the ship. It begins to feel like a prison instead of a safe refuge; I am captive and have no way of escape, nowhere to go, absolutely no alternative.

If I had my way, William and I would have started right then to cut logs and gather branches and make a lean-to in our spot, making a temporary home right out there on the shore. It would have been so easy. Our spot provided a perfect view of all the activity around us. The shore was comfortable. There were trees and rocks and solid ground. The fresh air was good for my mind and spirit and body. But Master Jones would never allow it, and William is not about to abandon the group and go off on our own. It would be foolish. I agree that the *Mayflower* is the safest place to be, but if I never had to leave the warmth and comfort of that quiet spot we found on shore, I would have been quite happy.

We took as much food as we could to have a small afternoon meal on the shore. I know that soon the men will start hunting and fishing, and we will have a marvelous supply of fresh meats to eat. From what I saw today, there are untold numbers of ducks and geese—an abundance of food. But for today it was still cheese and bread and few rations for all. At low tide some discovered barnacles and a supply of unknown seaweeds and mussels. I was a bit disgusted at the sight of it all, but several indulged. I am now thankful for my hesitation as it led many to a stomach illness.[24]

Before we left to go back to the ship, Elder Brewster led a small memorial service for Butten. That service may be the root cause of my feeling of exhaustion and disquiet this evening. It was truly a beautiful and simple tribute to his life. We carried out every one of his wishes, sang the psalms he wanted us to sing, read the scriptures he wanted us to read. I clung to his little cap all through the service for strength to make it through. I have decided to give that cap a special place in our home; I need to keep some reminder of him with me.

Again, it is so bittersweet to finally be here and not have him with us. His loss creates an empty feeling, a sadness with no words to express it. William is trying to comfort Dr. Fuller. He is still grieving this loss and desperately needs his family to arrive in the spring.

Just as Elder Brewster was saying his final words, a flock of twenty or so shore birds flew directly overhead and we watched as they landed near the shoreline and scurried about scouting for food. Their presence, at that precise moment, felt like a sonnet or a closing hymn. It was almost like Butten was there with us somehow. It was beautiful and encouraging and brought a much-needed sense of closure, a moment of hope and peace, a reminder that Butten may have left this life of limitations but has entered into the Lord's presence. He has entered a new dimension. He is safely home and at rest, in a much better place than we are.

Then darkness overtook us. We quietly left that beautiful spot on the shore and reluctantly boarded the small ship and returned to the *Mayflower*.

Tuesday, November 14

The name of the Lord is a strong tower: the righteous runneth into it, and is safe.
— Proverbs 18:10

Dear Jaqueline,

At sunset the sky exploded with colors. Pinks and creams streamed from the western horizon like pale colored ribbons trying to catch the impending dark from the east. Behind one of the softer tones of pink I could barely make out the moon, growing into her first quarter. Sadly, I don't think anyone noticed the beauty in the sky; they are preoccupied with tomorrow's exploration.

Sixteen men were chosen to explore the shore. William, Allerton, and Edward Tilley will be among them. They plan to search the entire east side of the bay for a riverfront, which is essential for the base of our settlement. Many don't think this exploration is a good idea. There are no people to be seen anywhere. Some are worried that hostile natives have somehow spotted us and now lie in wait to ambush the entire group.

Standish will lead the search. Standish has been touted for his experience as a soldier, but William is almost now convinced Standish hasn't any real idea of exactly what he is doing.[25] There were even whispers tonight that John Smith would have been a better leader after all. Smith's maps clearly show that the best waterway is to our northwest, but Standish insists he saw the mouth of a river when we first sailed into the harbor, so the plan is to explore the entire bayside stretch of land. Carver has given them explicit instructions to be cautious, and Stephen Hopkins will go in case they encounter Indians. They have unpacked the muskets and swords and what little armor we have.

All are a little on edge. I can't see anyone getting much sleep tonight.

Wednesday, November 15

Being confident of this very thing, that he which hath begun a good work in you will perform it until the day of Jesus Christ.
— Philippians 1:6

Dear Jaqueline,

The men left at dawn and I can tell you it's been a long day to endure. They rowed ashore in Master Jones's boat. That is to say, they were rowed as close to shore as possible. The boat ran aground several yards out, so the men, armor and all, had to wade through the tidal flat.

Several of us watched until they were out of sight. From my spot on the deck, I could barely make out the long, thin stretch of land to the east of our ship. It finally blended with sky and clouds, and I could no longer tell which was which.

The land from here to there appears desolate, scrubby, and completely unpopulated, and at the same time it holds a sense of promise with an abundance of trees near the shore. I picture what the trees will look like in full green and think this could indeed be a beautiful spot to build. I do so wish we were building homes in this weather. It's perfect. The mornings are chilly, but by midday the sun is high and temperatures fool us into thinking it's almost spring. I wonder if you're going to get this same unseasonably warm weather in Holland before winter sets in. I am at least thankful that the men have comfortable weather for exploring.

I prayed for many things as the men departed. Safety; food, if they can find any, for our sick and hungry; friendly encounters, if they have any encounters at all. We sang many psalms as they rowed ashore, and I sang out as bravely as I could, choking back my tears.

I refuse to let anyone know, but I will tell you, that I am terrified. At one point this morning I started literally shaking, and it wasn't from the cold, although it was damp and near freezing. What if William doesn't return? I don't think I've been apart from him for more than an afternoon or a morning since we were married. Master Jones and Governor Carver have stayed behind, so I know we will be safe, and I would most certainly have a place among this community of wonderful friends. But trying to make a life here without William? What a dreadful thought to consider. I can share these thoughts with only God and you. I know he will direct me if or when that time comes.

My initial thought is if William doesn't return, I will likely ride the *Mayflower* back with the crew and find my way home to you. Abandoning the group is hard to imagine, but at this point I can see no reason to stay if William is not here with me. My first responsibility, of course, would be to get back home to little John as soon as I possibly could. But would I be able to survive a journey back across the Atlantic? In the middle of winter? Oh Lord. I try not to think such thoughts, but they do creep in and send me into a mental spiral that is difficult to climb back out of.

It's warm enough now that I can stand in my spot on the deck all afternoon and stay until the sun sets. Then the temperatures drop, and the dark of night drives me below. I will continue this devoted search of the horizon for any sight of their boat until William returns. And if there is no sign of them, I will whisper my prayers to the heavens. That way, wherever they are, whatever trials they encounter, whether they be Indians or cold or hunger or fear, my God will meet their every need. I honestly don't know what else I can do, except trust my Lord for their safe return.

Thursday, November 16

Behold, I will do a new thing; now it shall spring forth; shall ye not know it? I will even make a way in the wilderness, and rivers in the desert.
— Isaiah 43:19

Dear Jaqueline,

Another long day to endure. The crew grows more and more anxious to make their journey back to England. It comes as no surprise; they are long overdue to finish their job here and return to their families. Thankfully Master Jones remains compassionate and insists that they can't yet abandon our group of men, women, and children.

I frittered away the early morning hours watching a thin mist rise in the trees along the shore. Just a simple morning fog, but it captivated me. Like white smoke, it rolled through barren tree limbs, gently making its escape to the treetops and then quietly disappearing into thin morning air. Gone.

It's incredible how different this harbor is compared to the busy harbors we've come through: ships of all sizes, uncontrolled comings and goings, horns blaring, dogs barking, chaos everywhere. And here—we are the only ship. It continues to give me an eerie feeling. The morning mist adds to the mystery of the scene. It's hard to imagine, but will this harbor be a major point of entry in some distant future day?

Browne and Priscilla were welcome faces on deck this morning. Priscilla's father is out with the explorers, and so is Goodman, so Browne is in charge of the two dogs. While we are anchored, the dogs have full run of the upper deck and take full advantage of it. They romp and chase one another in good sport. Their enjoyment of the fresh air did a great deal to cheer both Priscilla and me this morning.

Browne may be eight years older than Priscilla, but their friendship extends back to days in Dorking where they grew up not far from one another. Their tales of family relationships are comical. They share family tales, but I find them somewhat hard to follow. I'm not sure I have this right, but I think they told me Browne's older sister married a man whose mother worked with Priscilla's father as administer of her estate. Then the brother-in-law's sister purchased the Mullins family house before the family boarded the *Mayflower*. They laugh and joke about perhaps being related to one another. I'm glad Priscilla has a good friend.

I spent most of the afternoon with several women, also now without their husbands. We enjoyed reading and discussing the book of Acts and the story of Tabitha. We know so little of her story, but she is an amazing servant and mentor. There is never a mention of her having a husband or children, but it appears she worked relentlessly, actively supporting her community, and was known for good works and charitable deeds. She spent her entire life serving others with the talents God blessed her with. Her simple deeds and compassion toward others brought many into the Kingdom. Perhaps I need to rethink my plan if William doesn't make it back. I could be more like Tabitha.

This evening we clearly saw their fire down the shoreline—a prearranged signal that they are alive and well, and an answer to prayer. I am much relieved; I may sleep well tonight. They are to return tomorrow. How I long to hear all they have discovered.

Saturday, November 18

But they that wait upon the Lord shall renew their strength; they shall mount up with wings as eagles; they shall run, and not be weary; and they shall walk, and not faint.
— Isaiah 40:31

Dear Jaqueline,

Yesterday was a long, long day, but our men are safely home. Praise God! From sunup to sundown we searched the horizon, yet there was no sign of them. Master Jones and Governor Carver rowed to shore before dusk to look for any sign of them. It was well after dark when we finally heard voices over the water and clearly heard sounds of their boat approaching.

The men were weary, beyond tired, drenched from rain, grateful, and completely energized to be reunited with us. Their stories went on into the wee hours of the morning, describing in detail every experience. Stories of Indians they trailed for several miles along the shore. Stories of marching for what sounds like miles and miles and miles in that heavy armor. Stories of a fresh-water pond and fresh spring water William describes "as pleasant to drink as beer or wine!" They did find signs of civilized people—homes and cooking utensils and even what might have been a burial site. But they suspect that the people have moved further inland for the winter season. They saw cleared fields with stubble from previous plantings and brought back kernels of corn—yellow, red, and blue—that we can plant in the spring. Although they reached the river mouth and were encouraged by the findings there, they saved exploration of it for a separate journey. It is all a great encouragement, and we are blessed by their courageous efforts.

They are sleeping late this morning. I don't even know how to express my thanks for their safe return and their promising explorations. If William tells his story of being snagged in the deer trap one more time, I'll have to pinch him. My sides are sore from laughing about it, although praise God for this gift of something to laugh about in the midst of these most dreary circumstances. In a silly ceremony last night, they presented him with the infamous noose that trapped him. It is a pretty piece of rope indeed. I must have him write down the story for you. He will tell it so much better than me.[26]

Sunday, November 19

Yea, though I walk through the valley of the shadow of death, I will fear no evil: for thou art with me; thy rod and thy staff they comfort me.
— Psalm 23:4

Dear Jaqueline,

I haven't slept well since Butten died. I wake in the middle of most nights, restless. If I'm lucky, I finally fall back asleep before dawn. My strange dreams have ceased, but for the past couple weeks I lie there in the dark, replaying every aspect of his passing, remembering things he said, things he did, things that happened. I guess this ritual is my mind's way of processing it all.

Of all things I remember from that night, one of the most striking is that I expected Butten to recover. He had beaten the odds every other time he was down. The only thing that brings me peace is remembering how he was not afraid at all to die. I mean not at all. Maybe his difficult breathing on the night he died was a sign of anxiety, but for the most part he was calm and relaxed even though, all the while he was leaving us, passing into eternal life.

His death is a reminder of how short our time is here. One minute you can be here and the next minute gone. Precious and thin is the line between life and death.

The grief I'm experiencing feels like a thin line as well, but more like a thin layer of ice. I walk it, stepping gingerly, slowly, thoroughly aware that I could break through the ice at any moment. One minute I can be cautiously walking, and the next minute I can be down under, completely overcome by a wave of emotions and loss and struggle. The ice is thin, and there is no confidence in my grief walk.

Today is rainy, and the dark clouds are low and hanging. You'd think this kind of weather would be depressing, but instead, it's comforting in a way I can't describe well. Oddly the low clouds provide an abundance of God's presence, as if in lowering the clouds, he comes closer to me.

A couple days ago I finally asked God in my prayer time, "Please help me deal with this grief." Finally, this morning I awakened feeling rested with a sense of perfect peace. It's as if God has nourished me and restored my soul, helping me to see things from his perspective. I am so deeply thankful for my all-knowing, all-loving God. His rod and staff have comforted me and brought me across the valley of fear.

Monday, November 20

For the Lord Jehovah is my strength and my song; he also is become my salvation.
— Isaiah 12:2

Dear Jaqueline,

Another morning feeling rested and strong.
"Fear thou not; for I am with thee: be not dismayed; for I am thy God" (Isaiah 41:10). Those words comfort me today like a warm wool blanket. It's not that I've reached any amazing conclusions in dealing with my grief. However, I do know that in this process of trusting God and turning over the processing to him, I have gained a calmness and peace and am now completely confident that God is walking this path of grief with me. That's what brings me peace today.

I've also recognized that Butten's death caught me completely off guard. Poppa's death was different. I remember his death as almost a relief. With his health declining over several years, we had time to prepare and to know what to expect. Although not quite ready when his death approached, we were able to be strong, knowing he was going to a much better, much healthier place. And afterwards, although I felt lost for many days and did not know whom to turn to with my questions of even the simplest things in life, I finally regained my balance in the new normal of life without Poppa. I learned to take my eyes off the sorrow and put my hope in God. I put my life and my future in God's hands, trusting that he who sits on the throne of the universe would renew and restore my life. There was life with Poppa and then life without Poppa. The healing process was completely different.

I also make note here of a debt of gratitude to my Marys: Mary Brewster, Mary Allerton, and little Mary More. Like godsent angels, they help carry me in the weakest of my moments to this place of peace and acceptance.

Mary Brewster and Mary Allerton. . . These two have stood on either side of me as if flanking me, nurturing me in the struggle, the heartache, the questions, the fears. I am thankful for the wisdom of these two precious friends and for their ability to offer strength that only true friends can provide.

But little Mary has been my lifeline. Her constant companionship, her constant reminder that each day is new and that life is here and now, has been key to keeping my mind focused on moving forward each day. There are mornings when I've wanted nothing more than to pull the covers over my head and stow away for the day. It's been little Mary who pulled back the gray blanket of despair and dragged me out into the vivid colors of life again.

Yes, Butten is no longer with us, but I have little Mary and William; I have all of you and my sweet, sweet little John. Each of you needs me to be my best.

Tuesday, November 21

And he shall be like a tree planted by the rivers of water, that bringeth forth his fruit in his season; his leaf also shall not wither; and whatsoever he doeth shall prosper.
— Psalm 1:3

Dear Jaqueline,

The temperatures have dropped dramatically. We have six inches of white, wet snow on the upper deck and ice forming now on the water.

In spite of temperatures hovering at the freezing mark, the whales play hard by us every day, and watching them is greatly entertaining. They are huge—the bigger ones measure longer than our ship—but are slow and extremely docile, almost purposeful in every activity. For the most part they spend their day swimming around, likely looking for food but enjoying the calm waters of the bay.

Sometimes they lift their tails high above the water and hold their pose for a moment before descending deep. Occasionally one slaps its tail hard on the water as if sending a strong message to any nearby whale. Sometimes they dive so deep we can barely see them below the surface of the water, and then they suddenly resurface elsewhere. At times they jump high up into the air and hurl their enormous bodies into the water, creating a frightening splash. Thankfully they do that further out in the bay, so by the time the waves ripple in, only a soft rocking reaches us. Can you imagine if they felt threatened and did that close to our ship? I'm certain we would capsize.

Sometimes they lie completely motionless on the surface as if they're sleeping or resting, and I wonder how such an enormous creature can lie still and float. They are curious about us, at times coming close to the ship as if gathering intelligence to report back to the group. We've even seen them lift their heads above water as if to make eye contact or get a good glimpse of the deck. I imagine they are looking for food or maybe wondering if the boat is a predator to be wary of.

I wish I understood more about these creatures. Little John would be fascinated. Little Mary is thrilled and terrified all at the same time. When we hear the whales nearby, she insists on going to the deck with us, but William has to hold her in a certain way so she can bury her face in his shoulder at a moment's notice. William likes to tease her, and when the whales leap into the air, he pretends to leap into the air with them. She screams out as if terrified at the thought, and then they burst into laughter together.

Master Jones and one of the crewmates have experience hunting whales in Greenland. They are wishing for a harpoon! I would not be able to hunt these beautiful creatures.[27]

Wednesday, November 22

The Lord bless thee, and keep thee:
The Lord make his face shine upon thee, and be gracious unto thee:
The Lord lift up his countenance upon thee, and give thee peace.
— Numbers 6:24–26

Dear Jaqueline,

Every morning I find myself repeating this same list of prayers for little John. I think it's funny that the same list comes to my mind every day, but these are the things that I know God is helping him with. My prayers are not even requests. They're more like praises because I know God is already working on these things in his life.

I praise God for watching over him and keeping him safe, keeping him protected from all the evils that could pass his way today. I include praise for how he is growing healthy emotionally, physically, mentally, spiritually, and socially. I send up praise for how God is teaching him all he needs to learn about trusting the Lord, choosing to serve and follow him all the days of his life, till he finds his own identity, joy, strength, peace, and hope in Christ. I offer praise for how God is leading him even now to green pastures and pleasant boundaries that God has prepared in advance for him. I praise even now for how God will provide him with strong Christian friendships, strong Christian role models (which God is already providing in you), and a strong Christian spouse. Do you laugh at that? That I'm praying even now for his future wife? I think it's never too early. I trust God to bring one special woman into his life one day, and it never seems too early to pray for her, whoever and wherever she may be, that even she will grow up in God's protective hands.

It seems forever since I hugged his little body and inhaled a full breath of those soft, blond curls. Sometimes he would smell like outdoors and sweat, other times like the smell of fresh linens after his bath. Oh, how I miss him and all of you.

Saturday, November 25

Finally, brethren, whatsoever things are true, whatsoever things are honest, whatsoever things are just, whatsoever things are pure, whatsoever things are lovely, whatsoever things are of good report; if there be any virtue, and if there be any praise, think on these things.
— Philippians 4:8

Dear Jaqueline,

The shallop has been deemed seaworthy, so they are finalizing plans to launch Monday on another expedition, with even more men and the stronger boys this time. Thomas Rogers and his son; Edward Tilley; Elias Story; John Turner and his two sons; and Martin and his stepson Solomon. All the young boys are thrilled to participate in this adventure. I'm certain Butten would have been one of the first to volunteer.

Master Jones will be in charge, which I think is a bit comical. William isn't quite sure how that came to be. It's true that Master Jones has continued to voice concern for many days about getting us off the ship and settled. His crew is desperate to be on their way. And at the same time there has been this growing, and sometimes quite vocal, opposition to Standish and his, shall we call them, adventuresome ways. I think the men are tired of no clear direction or plan. Master Jones played his authority card and trumped the leadership role.[28] Anyway, we will be without him here, which is a bit concerning, but Elder Brewster and Governor Carver will stay behind again, although even that role is starting to wear a bit thin—staying behind while others explore, unendingly caring for the sick, watching over the women and children. Thankfully they continue to stay healthy in spite of it all. We can only hope the men will return with promising news of where to settle.

I am grateful we have a full day together tomorrow and am even more grateful that it's a full day of worship and prayer before they leave. But more than that, I am thankful that Monday will be another wash day, which will keep my mind occupied for several hours after the men leave.

Monday, November 27

For my thoughts are not your thoughts, neither are your ways my ways, saith the Lord.
For as the heavens are higher than the earth, so are my ways higher than your ways, and my thoughts than your thoughts.
— Isaiah 55:8–9

Dear Jaqueline,

Seeing the shallop in water today renewed my hope that God will grant us success in this journey. We applauded as the men pulled away from the *Mayflower*. Thirty-four men set out, including several of the crew who joined Master Jones in his boat at the last minute. They much prefer being in his company than staying behind with the women, children, and sick ones.

But the two boats had a rough go of it. It was difficult to watch. The wind picked up and seemed to throw them off course a bit. Temperatures started dropping, so those of us who stayed behind were driven below deck. We even had to put off laundry day, as it's not fit to be out there.

So here I am again, without William and without little John, and my thoughts become quite vulnerable, questioning what we are doing here and how we got here. At these times it's as if I fall into a deep hole of considerations and have to walk through the entire process—from the initial planning stages all the way up to the present. It seems to be the only way to climb out of my hole of questions and doubts.

My memories of those early planning conversations are starting to fade now with all that has happened, but I know there was never a question of whether William would go to America or not. He was always going. He felt an importance in the mission. And he still carries that burden. Even today, as they ventured out, he carries this massive responsibility and drive to establish a settlement, to do God's work here, no matter the cost.

We made the final decision to come through many long discussions and intense times of prayer. We had concerns about how much we could afford to pay, both for this trip and for future trips; we prayed about whether little John should stay behind and join us in the spring when a home was readied or whether I should stay behind with little John and both of us join William in the summer with the rest of the congregation. But with little John less than three years old, we weren't convinced he was up for the journey.

I clearly remember the turmoil in our discussions—conversations that kept me awake at night. I would replay them over and over and over in my mind as if hoping the decision would become obvious on its own. I weighed out scenarios and considered conditions of the voyage, the dangers of the wild, the hard work of establishing a community. I considered the reports of Jamestown and wondered, even then, whether William would have time to consider our needs and care for little John and me while meeting the needs of the church leadership. That's just it. Even back then I knew what would be expected of William. So why do I now wish for something he can't provide?

It's almost comical how I am here, again, going over all this in my mind. As if it were a bad decision that I can't let go of. But every time I review the planning and the decision, I always end up right back where I started—with a deep sense of conviction that I was to go and that we were to leave little John behind. I should also note that often, when I reflect on all that has happened, I am overcome by emotions at the thought of your immediate willingness and enthusiasm when asked to care for little John. You and Momma, without hesitation, stepped up to answer the task. How can I ever repay you? And would I have been willing to do the same? I'm not sure.

I can only imagine that the majority of the childcare is falling on your shoulders. I am praying daily that someone, maybe Bridget Robinson, is stepping in to help you as promised. I am also hopeful that by now you and others are finalizing plans to join us. That, in some small way, is what keeps me going day after day. I miss you all, terribly.

Wednesday, November 29

My sheep hear my voice, and I know them, and they follow me:
And I give unto them eternal life; and they shall never perish, neither shall
any man pluck them out of my hand.
— John 10:27–28

My dear Jaqueline,

What a day! Several of us were up all night with Aunt Susanna, and close
to noon today she gave birth to Peregrine. His name means "traveler to foreign lands," and quite the traveler he has already been.

When Aunt Susanna's contractions started late last evening, it was
Katherine Carver and her maidservant Dorothy who took charge. It's funny,
but I finally got to see a side of Katherine that I completely respect and like
quite well. It was almost a little shocking when she started barking out instructions, but I tell you—people listened. Carver and Uncle William were
sent to tend the sick and watch over Resolved, who was already asleep in his
bunk. With more than a third of our group out in exploration, Katherine ordered the remaining boys and men to move belongings and opened up quite
a bit of space for Aunt Susanna and her entourage of women.

Katherine has been a dear friend to Aunt Susanna for a long time but
has always been a bit difficult for me to get to know—so different from her
sister Bridget. While she can easily have friendly conversations during
teatime, she always has an air of distance, as if she can't step across some hidden barrier of family prominence into the world of the common people. Anyway, she was superb in action last night, and it was a pleasure to work as part
of her team. She never left Aunt Susanna's side, even into the wee hours of
the morning. She was a true saint in helping Aunt Susanna through every
difficult moment of the delivery. And she never stopped shouting out orders
until the baby had arrived and was safely swaddled in his mama's arms.

As I stood by and watched Peregrine take his first breath, I was overwhelmed again by the thin line between life and death. Here Butten passed
away not even a month ago, and now a new life steps in, as if to fill that void.
Is life a constant exchange of those that leave with those that arrive? The cycle
of death and life is truly fascinating—not in a morbid sense but in how
quickly our time on this earth passes. Some, like Butten, are here for only a
few short years. Those we encounter and spend our time with along the

way—is there rhyme and reason to it? It's all a complete mystery but I am more and more aware that God's sovereign hand rules over all of it; this knowledge gives me perfect peace, and I shouldn't worry about a thing.

Master Jones returned late this afternoon with ten overflowing bushels of corn seed, enough ducks and geese to last us several days, and more than a dozen sick men who needed immediate tending.[29] Two days of snow and temperatures much below the freezing mark obviously took a toll. This initial group of explorers appears numb to the core. They shared no good news of the areas they explored, no potential of a site for building.

William is not among them, so I am both anxious and thankful at the same time, assuming he is faring better than these. Master Jones pre-arranged a time tomorrow when he will return for the remaining eighteen men. They insisted on an extra day to explore the shoreline, and tonight they have the light of a full moon to help them make the most of their exploration.

Speaking of. . . I don't ever remember seeing a moon as big and wide and bright and full as the one that rose over the bay tonight. The sky was still full of lingering daylight when it appeared over the treetops, and the sight was breathtaking. Slowly it rose high above the trees, and the sky darkened to show off the celestial light. I love that the moon is not one flat circle of reflected light that rises idly in the night sky but instead an intricate mystery of dappled shades, gray and white and black. That little face of the cherub that I so clearly see in the full moon simply takes my breath away, and I have to look away in wonder and amazement. An additional blessing of this day.

I had another dream last night. I can still see it clearly in my mind. I was wading down a strongly flowing creek bed, taking careful, cautious steps down the edge, feeling my way along the rock bottom. The middle of the creek had larger boulders, and water flowed smoothly over the stones. The edge of the creek was beautiful, lined with large green fully leafed trees as if it were full summer. I don't remember the water being cold or hard to walk through, but I can picture it clearly rushing by, quickly flowing downstream. I am pretty sure the dream had something to do with Butten.

Thursday, November 30

And he said unto me, My grace is sufficient for thee: for my strength is made perfect in weakness. Most gladly therefore will I rather glory in my infirmities, that the power of Christ may rest upon me.
— 2 Corinthians 12:9

Dear Jaqueline,

A low, low day. Discouragement has tortured me all day long, and I wish William were here to lift me out of this hole. Why is his work out there more important than staying here with me? Why has God left me alone on this boat? What in the world are we doing with our lives? Why would we have left our safe home and family behind?

I have lost all interest and energy in connecting with anyone today. And I am not alone in this. Many of the passengers seem distant, as if we're a puzzle all broken apart, struggling to find a sense of purpose in all this. William says we will someday look back on this as a stepping-stone in the path of our lives, that one day we will look back and marvel at all we went through. I hope so.

I try to convince myself I need to make the most of this time. I should be preparing for the days ahead and getting a start on all the work that lies ahead of us. But my heart is not in it. I can't seem to pull myself out of these selfish thoughts of all the things I miss about home. I spent much of my day thinking about you and Momma and little John, remembering days of playing in the creek, teaching him to fish and skip rocks, looking for turtles and lizards and butterflies, soaking up every minute of life. But it goes deeper than that, as if I am thirsty for a deep drink of cool, refreshing water or whatever will make this all right again.

Here, there is no distracting three-year-old or family or job. All this time alone drives me to questions. And the questions become a spiral, starting with my worst fear and adding a coil in the spiral with each "what if" question.

For a while I went on deck for some fresh air and saw the sailors at work. They are a quiet team, each knowing and doing their job. And the questions start again—what would my job be if William doesn't return today? What if William doesn't return at all? Would I even be able to mentally accept that? He has been and is an amazing gift from God. How would I be able to go on without him? Everything would change. Would I be willing to stay here without him? I do have family ties to Uncle William and Aunt Susanna but I'm not sure that would keep me here. It seems that everything we are working toward is tied up with William. Does that mean I'm hiding behind William? Some women hide behind their husbands, but I don't believe I have that disposition. I am much too independent. But then why do these thoughts throw me into a torturous cycle when he's away?

I do believe that everything happens for a purpose. And I know God is using this time to teach me that he is the only one who truly matters in my life. If William doesn't return, I would have to somehow find the strength to figure out what next steps are best. I would to be willing to serve where Jesus needs me to. I pray that I would be, but I wonder.

There are many good and positive things around me, but most days I tend to lose focus of them. Even my three Marys can't seem to lift my spirits—Mary Brewster, my dearest friend, has a strong faith but struggles with her own difficulties—pressures of being the wife of our leading elder, the stress of raising boys. They require most of her energy and time. We occasionally get to sneak away to the upper deck for a sunset and get to exchange words of encouragement, but even then, I sense that her mind is saturated with preoccupations and that she is exhausted from the demands of her family.

My developing friendship with Mary Allerton is one of the true blessings of this journey. I love stepping in to help her and offer relief from the demands of her little ones, but her daily routine is so different from mine. I know that she needs my support, and I continue to provide that, but I long for time to connect with these women, and those opportunities are few and far between.

Little Mary is my constant daily companion. For her I can be a strong, trustworthy adult in her life. I hum to her and hold on to her; she crawls into my lap each night, and especially on these days when William is gone, little Mary is my encourager.

I praise God for getting me to look beyond my selfish thoughts today and focus on the blessings I have right here. I have renewed courage to be a light for God's Kingdom and renewed energy to run toward those who are truly broken, as Jesus did. I pray that God continues to enable me with his strength and courage to do the work he needs me to do.

Monday, December 4

Wait on the Lord: be of good courage, and he shall strengthen thine heart: wait, I say, on the Lord.
— Psalm 27:14

Dear Jaqueline,

We have had four days now of bitter argument—whether to start the building here or continue exploration. Time is of the essence, and I have no say-so in the matter. I am, however, grateful that they are keeping their exchange of words to the upper deck, so all we hear below are muffled bits and pieces.

Some want to stay here in the bay and settle in the land the Indians have cleared for planting. The pros: ponds of fresh water and plenty of fish and waterfowl. It is almost winter, and we shouldn't waste another day looking for a better place when there is no better place. Even more are now overcome with the sickness. Food is nearly gone. We have been anchored for almost a month and need to start building before it gets much colder.

Others say no. The cons: water along the shore is not deep enough for ships to come and go. Indians will return here in the spring and will not be pleased if we have taken over their settlement. There may be fresh water in ponds, but it will dry up in summer. Those against staying say we must continue to look for a suitable place.

Back and forth it goes. I know William feels strongly that we haven't found our promised land yet, and knowing him, he will win this argument.

In the midst of all that, Edward Thompson passed away today. He was Uncle William's servant, just a boy, coming of age. Uncle William is a bit mystified. He says Edward appeared to be so strong these last few days but apparently not strong enough to fight off the quickly spreading illness.

Jasper More's fever has escalated and burns intensely. It seems impossible to control. He now hardly seems to recognize our presence. Ellen, Richard, and little Mary are vigilant to stay by his side day and night.

We are all jarred by the sickening thought that death may become a regular visitor. What's scary is that we are not well prepared at all to battle whatever this is. Even Dr. Fuller is struggling to make sense of it.

Tuesday, December 5

But thou, O Lord, art a shield for me; my glory, and the lifter up of mine head.
— Psalm 3:3

Jaqueline,

William caught me racing in here today to write down the news for you. He says my obsession with writing down all the details of the day for you is a bit silly. But we barely escaped with our life today, so he has a better understanding of the importance of sharing these kinds of details.

As I make note of it, I hope we will look back on this one day and laugh. I am thankful it provides a bit of comic relief in the midst of our extreme circumstances. No harm was done, but there was a loud explosion and then men, women, and children running in *every* direction. It must have been either a very scary or a very comical sight—I'm not sure which!

Let me back up. It's true that Master Jones has been quite liberal with letting us move about the anchored ship, but some areas are strictly off-limits. And, to be honest, there are some areas that no one wants to go in. I have noticed Master Jones requires the steerage cabin to be completely clean. The floor is free of machines and ropes. All maps and documents are stored neatly in the shelves for immediate access if needed. But the sailors' cook room is completely disgusting. And from what little I've seen of the hold, it is a rather filthy encounter. Who in their right mind would even want to go in there? But then, I don't have the mind of a Billington boy.

Anytime their father is preoccupied with a task, the two Billington boys run rampant through the decks. They wanted a release of energy, I guess, but they seem to have an inclination for trouble. Somehow the boys got into the gun room. They confiscated powder and went back into their own family's area without being noticed.

First, we heard a sudden blast, and I immediately took cover in the bunk. Women screamed, children cried, men shouted, and sailors ran to and fro across the upper deck in a complete panic. Then a fire broke out, and it wasn't long before tall flames shot into the air, reaching for the highest point, and smoke filled the between deck. I didn't know what to grab first, but William said to leave it all behind, and we raced up the ladder with little Mary.

In spite of the bitter cold that unfortunately returned today, everyone moved quickly. A group of seven or eight men, including Governor Carver,

William, Winslow, and Standish naturally stepped into the role of. . . I'll call them responders in action. Their response is notable because we didn't nominate them for that role. No one spoke to them ahead of time about what to do whenever a crisis breaks out. But they do it. And they do it so well. Today they shouted orders, cleared the area, took immediate charge over the chaos, and brought the situation under control. They work well as a team, and today they came across as one voice of authority until the calm was restored and the fire was extinguished. I am so grateful for their natural abilities of directing a panicked crowd and their willingness to step into that role without being asked. I need to bring this to Elder Brewster's attention, to commend them for their actions.

In the end, no one was injured. The smoke cleared, but the stench of burnt wood and ropes is thick in the air. The responsible children were reprimanded, and we are all thankful for surviving another day. Once again, through God's mercy, we escaped a great danger without harm.[30]

Wednesday, December 6

Then shall the lame man leap as an hart, and the tongue of the dumb sing: for in the wilderness shall waters break out, and streams in the desert.
— Isaiah 35:6

Dear Jaqueline,

Our men set out early this morning. As soon as they raised sail, a sheet of freezing saltwater covered their coats with a thin glaze of ice. The seas are incredibly rough, and visibility was horrible. I watched from the upper deck for a couple minutes but could barely make out their boat in the horizontal sleet and freezing rain. Not a good day for exploring, and if we were not so desperate to find land, they would have postponed the trip.

Fewer men were able to go on this trip—many are still recovering from the last exploration. For the most part the men have been taking turns for these trips, but William has gone on every one of the explorations. He feels a strong obligation, an almost overwhelming sense of duty, to find the right place to build. He believes with God's help they will find our Canaan, so without hesitation he requested a spot on the team.

The group is half the size as last time out. This time Governor Carver, Standish, Winslow, Tilley and his brother Edward, Howland, and Hopkins and his servant Edward have gone, so I worry not about their safety. Our two pilots, Robert Coppin and Richard Clarke, are with them, and I am certain with their skills, plus the addition of our master gunner and three sailors, they will be in good hands and are sure to find a building spot. I am missing William more than usual today and wish he had stayed behind. I am desperate to share this news about Jasper with him.

Within a few hours of their departure this morning, sweet little Jasper's frail, tiny body finally gave up the fight. Katherine wonders if Jasper waited for Governor Carver to depart before letting down his display of strength and courage. Others say it's as if he were unable to deal with the stress of abandonment any longer. I am thankful that Jasper, like Butten, is now living free from pain, free from this earthly life, and enjoying the light of everlasting life. But Governor Carver and William will be so saddened to hear of this when they return. The loss of another young boy is especially devastating.

I know if he were here, William would find the right words to comfort Richard, Ellen, and little Mary. We are struggling to support them. It's one thing to lose their parents, but now they have lost a sibling as well. The three of them have been by Jasper's side every minute of these last few days. Their tight-knit group, now one less, will have to figure out how to continue without him. Their faith is strong, but the plight of these young ones is sad. It is one thing to deal with death as an adult; it is a completely different experience for a young child.

Master Jones has been most helpful today as the horror of death washed over all of us again. So many are ill. It brings a harsh and stunning awareness. Families cling tightly to one another now. Mothers hold their children close. Children are more subdued and more appreciative than normal. We are a mourning community, a desperate group of hungry, weary travelers wrapped in one tight circle of tears and sorrow.

All are affected by these events. All are changed. Not only have we come through a perilous and dangerous journey together, but now we experience together how precious life is, and we see firsthand, again, what a thin, thin line exists between this life and death.

It's a little odd to say it, but we no longer seem to be a community of Separatists and non-Separatists. We are a community of friends, supporting each other in life and death. The barriers that may have existed between us initially are all but gone, leaving a tie of honest friendship and a deep capacity for caring for one another.

I think of Priscilla—we are from different worlds, but she now looks to me for encouragement and sees me as a reliable adult, someone other than a parent, who can offer objective advice and counsel. And Sarah Eaton—she has quickly made friendships with many in our community but still relies on me to keep her connected to these other women.

I am even growing closer to some of the women from Leiden. Before this journey I never had any sort of friendship with Elizabeth Winslow. We had absolutely nothing in common. In fact, I never would have had the courage to approach her. Her family prominence established us in different social and daily life circles. But I admire her courage to join this venture to America, and that commonality removes every barrier that ever lay between us.

Like my William, her Edward has been pulled into the leadership circle. Many days we find ourselves side by side, her with little Ellen and me with little Mary. Yesterday when Katherine made some funny comment about the Governor, I glanced over at Elizabeth, and she had this big twinkle in her eye as if she knew I wanted to laugh out loud but didn't dare. She is kind and funny and smart. I'm amazed and thankful that she wants to be my friend.

Even Aunt Susanna. Years ago, when we all lived in Amsterdam, we had little opportunity to spend time together. But now that we're here we have many occasions to visit. She is a few years older than me, but that age difference doesn't seem to matter. While it is not the same as having you or Momma here, I count it a blessing to have someone here with shared family ties. Especially on days when I feel overwhelmed, Aunt Susanna lends a listening ear that helps me cope with fears and doubts. She is very busy with Resolved, and now Peregrine, but she is a wonderful confidante.

William has noticed, and commented to me on numerous occasions, how fortunate we are to have a cooperative group of women aboard the *Mayflower*. We each have different strengths but work well together as a team. We each have different personalities but are united through our circumstances and our bonds of faith. We are independent women, but we have learned to depend upon one another. And that is the only way we are possibly going to be able to cope with this tragic illness affecting so many and face the tough, nearly impossible challenges that lie ahead for us.

Once again God focuses my thoughts on his blessings and renews my courage.

One month later—
Sunday, January 7, 1621

Now the God of hope fill you with all joy and peace in believing, that ye may abound in hope, through the power of the Holy Ghost.
— Romans 15:13

Dear Jaqueline,

First of all, please accept my deepest condolences, to you, to your Momma, to little John, and to all of your family. I don't know how or when this news about Dorothy will reach you, but I know it will be devastating for all of you, as it has been here for us.

There are no words to express the depth of my sorrow at her passing. As you know, your Dorothy was like a sister to me, a forever friend. To lose her so unexpectedly and then have her brought back to life in these letters she has written to you is both heart-wrenching as well as an amazing blessing to me.

A few days after William came out of seclusion, he entrusted these letters into my keeping. It was a solemn moment between us, but I consider it a privilege indeed. I've read every one of them now and have soaked in every sweet morsel of inspiration and truth. But because I know these letters were intended for you, I will keep them safe here until you join us in the spring. I know how much Dorothy was looking forward to your arrival.

I pray these letters will be an encouragement to you, to your family, and to little John. They are like treasure. Dorothy's words bring great comfort, like a warm blanket to wrap up in. As I read them, I find myself wanting to tell her what parts I've laughed at, what parts struck me as odd—having no idea that she thought some of these things—and what parts resonated deep within me in agreement. But to have her words here without having her also leaves a strangely empty feeling. I'm sure you, of all, will understand that. I add here a note of my own so you may have a full record of all that happened in her passing.

December 7. Exactly one month ago today. I expect the seventh day of the month will be an intense hurdle for me from now on. That day was one of the darkest days I have faced. A lot of color left my life that day. The morning was foggy. Temperatures fell below freezing for the first time. Winds howled from the land to the west and swept across the waters with a bitterness unlike any cold we had experienced yet. Our group was completely on edge.

The team of explorers was out, but we had no word or sign of where they were or whether they were even alive. Many of our group were sick, and families were hungry. We were down to stale bread and cold mush. Worry settled in with the dark clouds; restlessness started to climb.

I know the ship was securely moored because I remember hearing the crew raise and lower the anchors that morning. Dorothy slipped away to the upper deck. She faithfully went every day to pray during William's journeys. She prayed for the group's safe return, for calmness and strength for us all, for wisdom and God's perfect plan to come to pass, and for God to provide for our every need. She was intensely faithful to her daily prayers with God.

There is no way to tell exactly what happened next. On any other day she would not have been alone. There were usually several others who would go on deck in the morning, but with the temperatures as cold as they were, she was by herself. Did she trip or lose her footing? With the ship anchored, did she climb to a higher post for better visibility? Was there an uneven plank in the deck? With the freezing temperatures and frozen salt spray and blowing winds, did she stumble? I know the entire upper deck was covered with a thin glaze of ice.

The crew heard her shouts for help. From down below I remember hearing racing footsteps across the upper deck. Those who could gathered to help, and I remember quite a bit of time lapsed while the team of men pulled Dorothy from the water. The waves were rough, and she kept getting pulled under. At one point she was under for quite some time, and we were terrified. But we finally got her on board, and many worked diligently to warm her, wrapping her tighter and tighter in blankets, talking to her, praying for her, fully expecting breath and that rosy cheek color to resume at any moment. But minutes passed, and the horror of what was happening came over us like a dark and heavy fog. We had no idea that frigid waters could drain a life so quickly. John Howland had fallen in the sea during our journey in rough waves, and he survived. We expected Dorothy to survive as well. But she did not.

It's a difficult memory to relive. What I remember most of those first few hours and days was an utter sense of helplessness and heaviness that took us captive. Her death was all I could think about every morning when I woke up, all through the day, and into the evening. I am sure I went about my responsibilities, but I couldn't focus. I struggled then, and I continue to struggle with redefining our circle without her here. Dorothy was our rock, our fearless helper, and our encourager. She was wrapped up in every detail of every plan of this entire adventure.

She made everything bright and beautiful from the first moment we became friends. I still hear her voice sometimes during the day, and I look but she's not there. At night I still lie awake wrestling with questions. How are we to go on without her? Why, like Moses, was she allowed to look over her promised land but not have a chance to enter it? Why would one who has been such a light and leader be taken? Did God take her now to spare her from some future experience? She was too young to leave us. She was much too vital to the success of our team.

First there was Butten, then Edward Thompson, and the day before Dorothy's accident the Carvers' servant Jasper passed. The day after Dorothy's death, we fell into desperate times. Sweet James Chilton, our oldest and arguably dearest passenger, died of the infection. Five sparkling lights suddenly out. Is this the dreadful end we will all come to? I know, of course, that there are no answers to my endless questions other than God simply saying that maybe I don't need to know the answers. Maybe it's enough to know that he's in control, whatever our circumstances. He reminds us that he is all we need.

For days we fretted of how to share this news about Dorothy with William. On the evening of December 12, the explorers returned. Busting on board with news of God's provision for a settlement location, they brought us a spark of life, a flicker of hope and purpose. But never will I forget William searching the crowd and Master Jones stepping forward to share the dreadful news. We watched the light fade from William's face, and he fell to his knees as life drained from his already exhausted body.

For days he seemed numb to the core. Their love was in the million little things. They were truly meant for each other. Although he speaks little of it, even to us, I know he has been dealt a tough, tough hand in life, having lost his parents, his sister, and his grandfather so many years ago and so early in life, and now he has lost his heart of hearts. For several days he was cared for in the small area we set up for the sick, either taken with sickness or grief— we were not sure. He has most recently been released, though; we are thankful for God's mercy on his life.

Winter has been ferocious. In late December, Mary Allerton gave birth to her stillborn. We lost countless friends and entire families to sickness and weakness, which loss created a level of sheer mental exhaustion. I know I will see all these friends again in heaven someday. I know I will enjoy the sweetest of reunions with Dorothy again. I know I haven't lost her because I know exactly where she is.

But I don't think heaven has seemed this close before. My father crossed over a few years ago, but this loss seems different. Dorothy was part of my every day. Dorothy and I had plans. We had things to do together. We were to build our homes next to one another. We were to grow old together. Her passing creates a large abyss that I am struggling to find my way. Even now I find it difficult to realize that she's gone. Just gone. I catch myself thinking of things I'd like to tell her. My eyes are permanently puffy. I cry every day. I know this is part of the grief, and I do trust that God has this all figured out.

But Jaqueline, I will tell you there are times when her spirit feels close by. It's like a feeling that comes in the breeze across the waters. There are times when I find myself waiting for her to speak my name and when her presence can almost be felt.

But I also know this time is the beginning of our hardships. Our men are now working with amazing purpose. Master Jones and his crew have delayed their journey home to help our crippled group get established. Their helpfulness is a blessing beyond words. We almost have the first few homes and storage sheds completed, so we will be off the boat soon. But with little to eat, the progress is slow. The women and sick have been forced to stay on the ship, and the close quarters are difficult.

At times I continue to simply feel lost in this fog that hangs over my mind. Winds howl outside, and I wonder how we will survive. I pray the fog will lift, the winds will be calm, and God will help me make sense of things again. I pray for a way to put one foot in front of the other today and tomorrow and the next day. I must do all I can now to keep this dream alive.

God sent me comfort in the words of the Bible, and I pray they will be a comfort to you as well:

Although the fig tree shall not blossom, neither shall fruit be in the vines; the labour of the olive shall fail, and the fields shall yield no meat; the flock shall be cut off from the fold, and there shall be no herd in the stalls:
Yet I will rejoice in the Lord, I will joy in the God of my salvation.
— Habakkuk 3:17–18

Blessed are they that mourn: for they shall be comforted.
— Matthew 5:4

Thou preparest a table before me in the presence of mine enemies: thou anointest my head with oil; my cup runneth over.
Surely goodness and mercy shall follow me all the days of my life: and I will dwell in the house of the Lord for ever.
— Psalm 23:5–6

*In a moment, in the twinkling of an eye, at the last trump: for the trumpet
shall sound, and the dead shall be raised incorruptible, and we shall be changed.*
— 1 Corinthians 15:52

*For now we see through a glass, darkly, but then face to face: now I know
in part; but then shall I know even as also I am known.*
— 1 Corinthians 13:12

*I will greatly rejoice in the Lord, my soul shall be joyful in my God; for he
hath clothed me with the garments of salvation, he hath covered me with the
robe of righteousness, as a bridegroom decketh himself with ornaments, and as
a bride adorneth herself with her jewels.*
— Isaiah 61:10

*Then spake Jesus again unto them, saying, I am the light of the world: he
that followeth me shall not walk in darkness, but shall have the light of life.*
— John 8:12

To my precious friend Dorothy, I say rest in peace, trusted friend and
companion. I know you are now dancing in glorious heavenly light and enjoying the presence of our Lord. I long to be there with you and will do my
best to carry on until that day.

Winter may be dreadful and uncertain, but it is upon us, and there is an
unsurmountable wave of work to be done. I will lean on God through each
day. I will trust that his plan and grace are sufficient. I promise to do all that's
possible to keep your memory alive. I promise to do my best to keep your
William at task and to help care for little John when he arrives in the spring.
I will hold tightly little Mary, who misses you unbearably. She lost first her
mother, then one of her brothers, and now you. All the loss creates a difficult
challenge for a young one. And yet she seems to have no fear of death. As she
sees it, you're not lost to us. Your life has blossomed into eternal glory.

Jaqueline, I vow to do all I can to deliver these letters into your hands in
hopes of providing peace and hope and comfort and healing to aching hearts.

Forever, your loving sister in Christ,

Mary Brewster

Closing Notes

On December 7 Dorothy May Bradford slipped over the side of the *Mayflower* and drowned in the icy waters of Cape Cod. There is no historic record of an eye-witness report of her death, so some have wondered whether her death was indeed an accident or of her choosing. Her faith-filled life seems overshadowed by speculation that her fall from the ship was intentional.[31]

Because all people are capable of depression, it is feasible that anyone who endured the hardships of such a voyage could fall into hopelessness, especially when coming face-to-face with a new life in a forsaken, desolate, bleak, and empty land. One could travel twenty-seven hundred miles equipped with drive and strong resolve and simply lose all sense of purpose after experiencing debilitating hardships and trials of hunger and disease and death. Depression is a heart-breaking and crippling disease, but I found no facts or records to suggest depression or suicide and believe it is hurtful for historians to color Dorothy's life with that sadness. I am convinced her death was an accident—a horrible, unexplainable, complete freak accident, with only God knowing the reason for the exact circumstances and exact timing to call her home.

William would have learned of Dorothy's passing upon his return from the third expedition on December 12. He never wrote about her death.

William and over fifty other passengers miraculously survived the first sickness and bitter winter of 1620/21. In April of 1621, William was elected governor of the established community following the sudden collapse and death of John Carver. William married the widow Alice Southworth, who sailed to Plymouth Colony in 1623 on the *Anne*. William was reelected governor of Plymouth Colony thirty-one times until 1657, the year of his death. William's faith, leadership skills, and survival instincts formed the inspiring foundation of Plymouth Colony.

William and Dorothy's son, John, eventually joined William in Plymouth Colony. John married Martha Bourne in 1650, took up residency in Duxbury, and later moved to Norwich, Connecticut.

Dorothy's mother and sister never made the journey to America.

The harsh winter of 1620/21 claimed the lives of 45 of the 102 *Mayflower* passengers, including James Chilton and his wife; Richard Clarke; John Crackstone (the father); Sarah Eaton; Edward Fuller and his wife; John Hooke; Christopher and Mary Martin; and Mary's son Solomon Prower; William Mullins; his wife, Alice; and his son, Joseph; Degory Priest; John and

Alice Rigsdale; Thomas Rogers; Rose Standish; Elias Story; Thomas Tinker, his wife, and son; John Turner and his two sons; Elizabeth Winslow; and William White.

John Alden became a prominent member of the Plymouth Colony. He married Priscilla Mullins in 1622 or 1623. Together they had ten children and eventually moved north to Duxbury. Priscilla died in 1680, and John died in 1687 at the age of 89.

Mary Allerton died the first winter. Her husband, Isaac, and their children lived for many years in Plymouth Colony. Isaac's sister, Sarah, arrived in 1623 on the *Anne* with her new husband and two daughters. Isaac later married Fear Brewster in 1624.

The Billington family lived through the first winter, but young John Billington died around 1627. In 1630 John, the father, was executed for killing a man. A few years later his wife Eleanor was found guilty of slander and was sentenced to sit in the stocks and be whipped. Francis Billington married and raised a family in Plymouth Colony, later moving to Middleboro.

Mary Brewster was one of only five women who survived the first winter. She died in Plymouth Colony in 1627. Elder Brewster and his children lived many years in Plymouth Colony. His oldest son, Jonathan, arrived in 1621 on the *Fortune*; his two oldest daughters, Patience and Fear, arrived in 1623 on the *Anne*.

Peter Browne lived in Plymouth until 1633 when became ill from a sickness that spread throughout the colony.

Governor Carver died unexpectedly in April 1621. His wife, Katherine, died six weeks later. Their servant Desire Minter returned to England in 1621.

Mary Chilton married John Winslow who arrived in 1621 on the *Fortune*. They had ten children and resided in Plymouth Colony for many years eventually moving to Boston.

After his father died in the first winter, young John Crackstone moved in with the Allerton family. John later died around 1627.

Francis Eaton married the Carver's servant Dorothy after his first wife died. Francis died in the sickness of 1633. His son Samuel eventually moved to Duxbury where he married and raised a family.

Dr. Fuller's wife, Bridget, eventually joined him in Plymouth Colony. He raised his young nephew Samuel after Edward Fuller and his wife died. Dr. Fuller died in the sickness of 1633.

John Goodman is known for having suffered from frostbite in the first winter.

Elizabeth and Stephen Hopkins lived many years in Plymouth Colony with their children.

John Howland married Elizabeth Tilley, daughter of John and Joan Tilley. They had ten children, and John Howland had several brothers who also came to America.

Edward Leister stayed in Plymouth for a time then moved to Jamestown, Virginia.

Of the More children, only Richard survived the first winter. Ellen and Mary both died on unrecorded dates.

After his father died in the first winter, Joseph Rogers moved in with the Bradford family. Joseph later moved to Duxbury and then to Eastham.

Myles Standish made many contributions to the establishment of Plymouth Colony. He remarried in 1623 and eventually moved to Duxbury.

Agnes Tilley and her husband, Edward, both died soon after the *Mayflower* arrival. Their niece, Humility Cooper, returned to England. Their nephew, Henry Sampson, stayed to live in Plymouth Colony. Edward's brother, John, and John's wife, Joan, also died soon after the arrival.

Susanna White married Edward Winslow in 1621, and they raised Resolved and Peregrine in Plymouth Colony.

On April 5, 1621, Master Jones and the crew left Plymouth Colony to return to England. The *Mayflower* arrived back home on May 6, in half the time of the original journey.

For several years the Pilgrims of Plymouth Colony awaited the arrival of Pastor Robinson and the rest of their congregation from Leiden, but the departure for most was delayed. Pastor Robinson became ill in 1625 and died. His oldest son, Isaac, joined the Pilgrims in Plymouth Colony in 1631 aboard the *Lion*.

At the time of this publication, it is estimated that more than thirty-five million individuals living today are direct descendants of the *Mayflower* passengers.[32]

While many of Dorothy's *Mayflower* companions were buried on Burial Hill in Plymouth, Massachusetts, her burial place is unknown and unmarked. She was, however, honored with two memorial stones, both located in Provincetown, Massachusetts: one at the Winthrop Street Cemetery and the other at the Mayflower Passengers Who Died at Sea Memorial.

Bibliography

A Sixteenth-Century Anthem Book. London: Oxford University Press, 1960.

Ames, Azel. *The May-Flower and Her Log, Complete: July 15, 1620–May 6, 1621, Chiefly from Original Sources.* Boston: Houghton, Mifflin, 1907. Project Gutenberg. Updated August 24, 2016. http://www.gutenberg.org/files/4107/4107-h/4107-h.htm.

Baker, Peggy M. "The Plymouth Colony Patent: Setting the Stage." Pilgrim Society & Pilgrim Hall Museum, 2007. https://pilgrimhall.org/pdf/The_Plymouth_Colony_Patent.pdf.

Bradford, William. *Of Plymouth Plantation.* Edited by Harold Paget. Mineola, NY: Dover Publications, 2006.

"Dorothy (May) Bradford, 'Mayflower Passenger.'" Geni. Updated April 25, 2019. https://www.geni.com/people/Dorothy-May-Bradford-Mayflower-Passenger/6000000001643820277.

Johnson, Caleb H. *The Mayflower and Her Passengers.* Bloomington, IN: Xlibris Corporation, 2006.

———. MayflowerHistory.com. Accessed May 5, 2020. http://mayflowerhistory.com.

Mayo, Melanie. "Are You One of 35 Million Mayflower Descendants? Here's How to Find Out." Family History Daily. Accessed May 15, 2020. https://familyhistorydaily.com/genealogy-help-and-how-to/are-you-one-of-35-million-mayflower-descendants-heres-how-to-find-out/.

Philbrick, Nathaniel. *Mayflower: A Story of Courage, Community, and War.* New York: Penguin Group, 2006.

Plimoth Plantation, Peter Arenstam, John Kemp, and Catherine O'Neill Grace. *Mayflower 1620: A New Look at a Pilgrim Voyage.* Washington, DC: National Geographic Society, 2007.

"Three Primers Put Forth in the Reign of Henry VIII." Oxford: University Press, 1834. Internet Archive. Accessed May 5, 2020. https://archive.org/details/threeprimersputf00unknuoft/page/476/mode/2up.

Wikipedia. "List of *Mayflower* Passengers." Last modified April 23, 2020. https://en.wikipedia.org/wiki/List_of_Mayflower_passengers.

Wikipedia. "Richard More (*Mayflower* Passenger)." Last modified March 6, 2020. https://en.wikipedia.org/wiki/Richard_More_(Mayflower_passenger).

Winslow, Edward. *Mourt's Relation: A Journal of the Pilgrims at Plymouth, 1622, Part I.* Plymouth Colony Archive Project. Accessed May 5, 2020. http://www.histarch.illinois.edu/plymouth/mourt1.html.

Endnotes

[1] *Page vii:* The Puritans felt that the Church of England was becoming too much like the Catholic Church of Rome. They did not agree that the church needed a hierarchy of bishops and archbishops or that the king of England should be the head of the church. They believed that only Christ could rule over the church. The Puritans supported a simple form of worship centered on a sermon and few rituals.

[2] *Page viii:* Establishment of the Jamestown colony in Virginia—England's first foothold in the New World—proved to be dangerous and difficult. From 1606 to 1609, the Jamestown settlers faced a lack of supplies, lack of fresh water, disease, conflicts with neighboring Indians, and extreme weather. The winter of 1609 became known as the Starving Time when approximately 80 percent of existing settlers died of either disease or starvation. By spring of 1610, all remaining settlers were set to abandon, but fresh supplies arrived from England, breathing new life into the dying colony and finally providing it a chance to grow and flourish.

[3] *Page ix:* Johnson, MayflowerHistory.com.

[4] *Page 3:* Dorothy May was born in Wisbech, Cambridgeshire, England. In the early 1600s, her family moved from England to Amsterdam, where she met and married William Bradford in 1613.

[5] *Page 5:* The book of hours was a common Christian devotional book in the 1600s.

[6] *Page 5:* William Brewster was constantly under surveillance by both British and Dutch authorities but managed to evade authorities by staying in hiding. Brewster came out of hiding in time to join the congregation before they sailed to North America.

[7] *Page 9:* "Three Primers Put Forth in the Reign of Henry VIII."

[8] *Page 12:* In his early teens, William Bradford moved from his uncle's home in Austerfield to join the Separatist congregation of Pastor John Robinson in Scrooby. In 1607 the congregation, facing persecution from the English government, made secret plans to escape to Holland, which offered more tolerance for their religious practices. Their initial attempt by boat was in the middle of the night, but they were betrayed by the ship's captain. Seven of the leaders were put in prison to face trial. Eventually the congregation found another ship to ferry them to Holland. Bradford lived with the Brewster family until he turned twenty-one and was able to buy property of his own.

[9] *Page 17:* Thomas Weston was a London merchant who organized

financial backing for the colonists. Christopher Martin was a Londoner assisting John Carver and Robert Cushman with purchasing supplies. Cushman was a key business agent for the Leiden congregation. He was a passenger on the *Speedwell* but became ill while the ship was in port in Dartmouth.

[10] *Page 26:* "Our victuals will be half eaten up, I think, before we leave the coast of England, and if our voyage last long we shall not have a month's victuals when we arrive." Bradford, *Of Plymouth Plantation*, 39.

[11] *Page 28:* "And have her mended, which accordingly was done, at great expense and loss of time and a fair wind." Bradford, *Of Plymouth Plantation*, 38.

[12] *Page 28:* "But it was partly due to the cunning and deceit of the captain and his crew, who had been hired to stay a whole year at the Settlement, and now, fearing want of victuals, they plotted this stratagem to free themselves, as was afterward confessed by some of them." Bradford, *Of Plymouth Plantation*, 39.

[13] *Page 31:* John Carver and Robert Cushman obtained a patent from the Virginia Company of London. This gave the Separatists permission to attempt a settlement. Last-minute changes were made to the terms and conditions of the venture, which upset many of the church leaders. London merchants would get to keep half of the housing and lands when the company was liquidated. The agreement allowed the settlers only one day per week off from labor instead of the previously agreed upon two days. This would be a considerable hardship since their day off would be Sunday and they could not work on Sunday for their personal benefit.

[14] *Page 31:* William Ring and Deacon Thomas Blossom had been aboard the *Speedwell* but were among the passengers who did not continue when the *Speedwell* was deemed unseaworthy.

[15] *Page 38:* "Charles Banks noted that there was a William Mullins who was called before the Privy Council in August 1616, and held for a period of time for an unrecorded reason. He speculates that perhaps William Mullins was involved in some kind of religious controversy that might hint at why he decided to join with the Pilgrims on their voyage to America." Johnson, *Mayflower and Her Passengers*, 194.

[16] *Page 56:* "There was an insolent and very profane young man,—one of the sailors, which made him the more overbearing,—who was always harassing the poor people in their sickness, and cursing them daily with grievous execrations, and did not hesitate to tell them that he hoped to help throw half of them overboard before they came to their journey's end. If he

were gently reproved by any one, he would curse and swear most bitterly. But it pleased God, before they came half seas over, to smite the young man with a grievous disease, of which he died in a desperate manner, and so was himself the first to be thrown overboard. Thus his curses fell upon his own head, which astonished all his mates for they saw it was the just hand of God upon him." Bradford, *Of Plymouth Plantation*, 41.

[17] *Page 72:* "One of the main beams amid-ships was bent and cracked, which made them afraid that she might not be able to complete the voyage. So some of the chief of the voyagers, seeing that the sailors doubted the efficiency of the ship, entered into serious consultation with the captain and officers, to weigh the danger betimes and rather to return than to cast themselves into desperation and inevitable peril. Indeed there was great difference of opinion amongst the crew themselves. They wished to do whatever could be done for the sake of their wages, being now half way over; on the other hand they were loth to risk their lives too desperately. But at length all opinions, the captain's and others' included, agreed that the ship was sound under the water-line, and as for the buckling of the main beam, there was a great iron screw the passengers brought out of Holland, by which the beam could be raised into place; and the carpenter affirmed that with a post put under it, set firm in the lower deck, and otherwise fastened, he could make it hold." Bradford, *Of Plymouth Plantation*, 41.

[18] *Page 79 :* There is no historical reference for this story of a sailor approaching the Pilgrims about the gospel, but the following is recorded in Bradford, *Of Plymouth Plantation*, 226: "Mr. Alden was hired at Southampton as a cooper. Being a likely young man, he was desirable as a settler; but it was left to his own choice to stay here [in America] or return to England; he stayed, and married Priscilla Mullins."

[19] *Page 97:* The Thirty Years' War took place in central Europe from 1618 to 1648. The Eighty Years' War took place between the Netherlands and Spain between 1568 and 1648.

[20] *Page 105:* Cape Cod. "A word or two, by the way, of this Cape. It was first thus named by Captain Gosnold and his people in 1602, because they caught much of that fish there; and afterwards was called Cape James by Captain Smith; but it retains the former name among seamen." Bradford, *Of Plymouth Plantation*, 42.

[21] *Page 107:* "The point where they first met with those dangerous shoals they called Point Care, or Tucker's Terror; but the French and Dutch to this day call it Malabar." Bradford, *Of Plymouth Plantation*, 42.

[22] *Page 109:* "'The Pilgrims sailed, landed outside of the jurisdiction of Jamestown and the Virginia Company of London (being north of northern New Jersey). They landed instead in the territory newly under the jurisdiction of the Council for New England. Since they had no legal 'paper' giving them permission to settle where they had landed or to construct a government, the Pilgrims drew up the Mayflower Compact as a personal, interim agreement. It governed the conduct of the settlers and was to remain an embodiment of the guiding principles for Plymouth Colony, but had no force in law as recognized by any outside authority.

"When the *Mayflower* returned to England in April of 1621, the Pilgrims sent back a request for another patent for a particular plantation. They asked, in effect, for permission to remain where they already were. This time, the request went to the newly established Council for New England, which had jurisdiction over the Plymouth area. Incorporated on November 3, 1620, under the name of 'The Council Established at Plymouth, in the County of Devon, for the planting, ruling, ordering, and governing of New England in America,' the corporation consisted of 40 patentees. . . .

"The Pilgrims' request was granted in 1621 with the document known as the Second Peirce Patent." Baker, "Plymouth Colony Patent."

[23] *Page 115:* "Having brought a large shallop [an open boat that could be both rowed and sailed] with them from England, stowed in quarters in the ship, they now got her out, and set their carpenters to work to trim her up; but being much bruised and battered in the foul weather they saw she would be long mending." Bradford, *Of Plymouth Plantation,* 44.

[24] *Page 118:* "We found great mussels, and very fat and full of sea-pearl, but we could not eat them, for they made us all sick that did eat, as well sailors as passengers; they caused to cast and scour, but they were soon well again." Winslow, *Mourt's Relation.*

[25] *Page 119:* "Standish was full of martial pugnacity, but he had no idea where he was leading them." Philbrick, *Mayflower,* 59.

[26] *Page 124:* "As we wandered we came to a tree, where a young sprit was bowed down over a bow, and some acorns strewed underneath. Stephen Hopkins said it had been to catch some deer. So as we were looking at it, William Bradford being in the rear, when he came looked also upon it, and as he went about, it gave a sudden jerk up, and he was immediately caught by the leg. It was a very pretty device, made with a rope of their own making and having a noose as artificially made as any roper in England can make, and as like ours as can be, which we brought away with us." Winslow, *Mourt's Relation.*

[27] *Page 129:* "And every day we saw whales playing hard by us, of which in that place, if we had instruments and means to take them, we might have made a very rich return, which to our great grief we wanted. Our master and his mate, and others experienced in fishing, professed we might have made three or four thousand pounds worth of oil; they preferred it before Greenland whale-fishing, and purpose the next winter to fish for whale here." Winslow, *Mourt's Relation.*

[28] *Page 131:* "On Monday, November 27, yet another exploring expedition was launched, this time under the direction of Christopher Jones. As the master of the Mayflower, Jones was not required to assist the Pilgrims in their attempts to find a settlement site, but he obviously thought it in his best interests to see them on their way." Philbrick, *Mayflower,* 65.

[29] *Page 135:* "When we came to the creek we saw the canoe lie on the dry ground, and a flock of geese in the river, at which one made a shot and killed a couple of them, and we launched the canoe and fetched them and when we had done, she carried us over by seven or eight at once. This done, we marched to the place where we had the corn formerly, which place we called Cornhill, and digged and found the rest, of which we were very glad. We also digged in a place a little further off, and found a bottle of oil. We went to another place which we had seen before, and digged, and found more corn, viz. Two or three baskets full of Indian wheat, and a bag of beans, with a good many of fair wheat ears. Whilst some of us were digging up this, some others found another heap of corn, which they digged up also, so as we had in all about ten bushels, which will serve us sufficiently for seed. And sure it was God's good providence that we found this corn. . . . Whilst we were in this employment, foul weather being towards, Master Jones was earnest to go aboard, but sundry of us desired to make further discovery and to find out the Indians' habitations. So we sent home with him our weakest people, and some that were sick, and all the corn, and eighteen of us stayed still, and lodged there that night, and desired that the shallop might return to us next day." Winslow, *Mourt's Relation.*

[30] *Page 140:* "The 5th day, we, through God's mercy, escaped a great danger by the foolishness of a boy, one of Francis Billington's sons, who, in his father's absence, had got gunpowder and had shot a piece or two, and made squibs, and there being a fowling-piece charged in his father's cabin, shot her off in the cabin; there being a little barrel of powder half full, scattered in and about the cabin, the fire being within four feed [sic] of the bed between the decks, and many flints and iron things about the cabin, and

many people about the fire, and yet, by God's mercy, no harm done." Winslow, *Mourt's Relation*.

[31] *Page 150:* Johnson, MayflowerHistory.com.

[32] *Page 152:* Mayo, "Are You One of 35 Million Mayflower Descendants?"